TESTAMENTS OF COURAGE

Selections from Men's Slave Narratives

by Mary Young and Gerald Horne

The African-American Experience
FRANKLIN WATTS
New York / Chicago / London / Toronto / Sydney

Chapter opening photograph courtesy of The Charleston Museum,
Charleston, S.C. Depicted is a "slave hire badge" worn by a slave
artisan whose labor had been sold, or "hired out," by his owner.
"Slavery for hire" was regulated by "badge laws" which required
that the place and year of issue, the trade, and the serial number
be imprinted on a thin piece of copper. Only those artifacts used
in Charleston, South Carolina survive today.

Library of Congress Cataloging-in-Publication Data

Testaments of courage : selections from men's slave narratives / by
Mary Young and Gerald Horne.
p. cm.
Includes bibliographical references and index.
ISBN 0-531-11205-5
1. Slaves—United States—Biography. [1. Slaves.] I. Young, Mary,
1940–   . II. Horne, Gerald.
E444.T37 1995
973' .0496073' 00922—dc20
[B]
95-1766 CIP AC

Contents

Introduction

The earliest and most popular slave narratives in the United States emerged in the eighteenth century with the works of Olaudah Equiano and Briton Hammon. *The Interesting Narrative of Olaudah Equiano*, published in 1789, was wildly popular, selling thousands of copies in English, German, and Dutch; as the Civil War approached in 1861, it was still selling briskly. Equiano was born in 1745, the son of a chief in West Africa. In often moving detail, he recounted his odyssey that took him to the Caribbean, Georgia, and Pennsylvania.

Briton Hammon's narrative, which was published in Boston in 1768, was not and has not been as popular as Equiano's. Hammon, strikingly, placed in the title of his work the fact that he was a "Negro Man." His tale of travail stretched from Boston to Florida to London.

The abolitionists of the nineteenth century believed that if people in the North knew of the horrors of slavery they would demand its end.

Talks by escaped slaves and the publication of slave narratives were sponsored by abolitionist groups in order to inform the public about the evils of slavery. Frederick Douglass, who joined the abolitionists soon after his escape to freedom, explains in his narrative that he wrote his account because some people who heard his antislavery lectures doubted that he had been a slave. As the struggle to end slavery intensified and the movement grew in numbers after the 1830s, an increasing number of slave narratives continued to appear until the Civil War.

Slave narratives followed a similar form, describing the author's suffering on the plantation, the terrible conditions the slaves endured, and the author's successful escape North. Some of the narratives were dictated to others, since slaves were forbidden to learn to read and write and therefore could not pen their own biographies. Exceptional slaves taught themselves to read and write and could write their own narratives, as did Frederick Douglass and William Wells Brown. Learning clandestinely to write was an impressive aspect of the slave's heroic adventure.

A new period in the slave narrative arose in the twentieth century as anthropologists and folklorists compiled narratives based on research and on interviews with former slaves. The continuing relevance and popularity of the slave narrative was confirmed when President Franklin Delano Roosevelt, as a way to combat unemployment during the Depression years of the 1930s, initiated an oral-history program as part of the Works Progress Administration (WPA). Writers and folklorists were sent into Deep South communities to take down the stories of surviving ex-slaves. These accounts provide some of the most richly detailed slave narratives.

Of course, by the 1930s many of those being interviewed were in their seventies or older. These accounts, at best, tell us what slavery was like during its dying days but do not tell us much by way of direct testimony about earlier periods. After all, by 1850 enslavement of Africans had been going on for well over two hundred years.

In addition, some have questioned the validity of relying on the precise recollections of people speaking of what had occurred sixty years earlier. Who among us can recall with precision what happened last week, say these critics, not to mention what happened decades ago?

Nevertheless, it would be a mistake to dismiss these often riveting, frequently graphic accounts. Their memories about diet, housing, kinds of gardens, and the like, are corroborated by other sources, such as archeological research. Their recollections about techniques of brutality used by slave owners are also corroborated by other accounts, such as recently discovered diaries kept by slave-owning families.

These narratives compiled in the 1930s take up tens of thousands of pages; scores of volumes of these accounts have been published. They remain one of our most enlightening sources about the nature and experience of slavery. These narratives are the chief way we can know what slavery meant to the slaves themselves.

—Gerald Horne

Louis Asa-Asa
1831

The *Narrative of Louis Asa-Asa, A Captured African*[1] is an account written by a rescued African in England of the raiding and capture of Africans for the slave trade.

It is necessary to explain that Louis came to this country about five years ago in a French vessel called the Pearl. She had lost her reckoning and was driven by stress of weather into the port of St. Ives, in Cornwall. Louis and his four companions were brought to London upon a writ of habeas corpus at the instance of Mr. George Stephen; and, after some trifling opposition on the part of the master of the vessel, were discharged by Lord Wynford. Two of his unfortunate fellow sufferers died of the measles at Hampstead; the other two returned to Sierra Leone; but poor Louis, when offered the choice of going back to

Africa, replied, "me no father, no mother now; me stay with you." And here he has ever since remained; conducting himself in a way to gain the goodwill and respect of all who know him. He is remarkably intelligent, understands our language perfectly, and can read and write well.

—Mr. George Stephen

The Negro Boy's Narrative.

My father's name was Clashoquin; mine is Asa-Asa. He lived in a country called Byela, near Egie, a large town. Egie is as large as Brighton; it was some way from the sea. I had five brothers and sisters. We all lived together with my father and mother; he kept a horse, and was respectable, but not one of the great men. My uncle was one of the great men of Egie: he could make men come and work for him: his name was Otou. He had a great deal of land and cattle. My father sometimes worked on his own land, and used to make charcoal. I was too little to work; my eldest brother used to work on the land; and we were all very happy.

A great many people, whom we call Adinyes, set fire to Egie in the morning before daybreak; there were some thousands of them. They killed a great many, and burnt all their houses. They staid two days, and then carried away all the people whom they did not kill.

They came again every now and then for a month, as long as they could find people to carry away. They used to tie them by the feet, except when they were taking them off, and then they let them loose; but if they offered to run away, they would shoot them. I lost a great many friends and relations at Egie; about a dozen. They sold all they carried away, to be slaves. They took away brothers, and sisters, and husbands, and wives; they did not care about this. They were sold for cloth or gunpowder, sometimes for salt or guns; sometimes they got four or five guns for a man; they were English guns, made like my master's that I clean for his shooting. The Adinyes burnt a great many places besides Egie. They burnt all the country wherever they found villages; they used to shoot men, women, and children, if they ran away.

They came to us about eleven o'clock one day, and directly they came they set our house on fire. All of us had run away. We kept together, and went into the woods, and stopped there two days. The Adinyes then went away, and we returned home and found every thing burnt. We tried to build a little shed, and were beginning to get comfortable again. We found several of our neighbours lying about wounded; they had been shot. I saw the bodies of four or five little children whom they had killed with blows on the head. They had carried away their fathers and mothers, but the children were too small for slaves, so they killed them. They had killed several others, but these were all that I saw. I saw them lying in the street like dead dogs.

In about a week after we got back, the Adinyes returned, and burnt all the sheds and houses they had left standing. We all ran away again; we went to the woods as we had done before.—They followed us the next day. We went farther into the woods, and staid there about four days and nights; we were half starved; we only got a few potatoes. My uncle Otou was with us. They called my uncle to go to them; but he refused, and they shot him immediately: they killed him. The rest of us ran on, and they did not get at us till the next day. I ran up into a tree: they followed me and brought me down. They tied my feet. I do not know if they found my father and mother, and brothers and sisters: they had run faster than me, and were half a mile farther when I got up into the tree: I have never seen them since.—There was a man who ran up into the tree with me: I believe they shot him, for I never saw him again.

They carried away about twenty besides me. They carried us to the sea. They did not beat us. They only killed one man, who was very ill and too weak to carry his load. They made all of us carry chickens and meat for our food; but this poor man could not carry his load, and they ran him through the body with a sword.—He was a neighbour of ours. When we got to the sea they sold all of us, but not to the same person. They sold us for money; and I was sold six times over, sometimes for money, sometimes for cloth, and sometimes for a gun. I was about thirteen years old. It was about half a year from the time I was taken, before I saw the white people.

We were taken in a boat from place to place, and sold at every place we stopped at. In about six months we got to a ship, in which we first saw white people: they were French. They bought us. We found here a great many other slaves; there were about eighty, including women and children. The Frenchmen sent away all but five of us into another very large ship. We five staid on board till we got to England, which was about five or six months. The slaves we saw on board the ship were chained together by the legs below deck, so close they could not move. They were flogged very cruelly: I saw one of them flogged till he died; we could not tell what for. They gave them enough to eat. The place they were confined in below deck was so hot and nasty I could not bear to be in it. A great many of the slaves were ill, but they were not attended to. They used to flog me very bad on board the ship: the captain cut my head very bad one time.

I wish the king of England could know all I have told you. I wish it that he may see how cruelly we are used. We had no king in our country, or he would have stopt it. I think the king of England might stop it, and this is why I wish him to know it all. I have heard say he is good; and if he is, he will stop it if he can. I am well off myself, for I am well taken care of, and have good bed and good clothes; but I wish my own people to be as comfortable.

Louis Asa-Asa
London,
January 31, 1831

Moses Roper
1838

Moses Roper was probably the first ex-slave to receive publicity as a fugitive who fled to England to escape bondage. His *A Narrative of Moses Roper's Adventures and Escape from American Slavery; with a Preface by Reverend T. Price*[2] contradicts the myth that mulattoes always led a privileged slave life.

Moses Roper begins his narrative with an account of his difficulties in slavery because he was a mulatto.

> I was born in North Carolina, in Caswell county, I am not able to tell in what year or month. What I shall relate is, what was told me by my mother and grandmother. A few months before I was born, my father married my mother's young mistress. As soon as my father's wife heard of my birth, she sent one of my mother's sisters to see whether I was white or black, and when my aunt had

seen me, she returned back as soon as she could, and told her mistress that I was white, and resembled Mr. Roper very much. Mr. R's wife being not pleased with this report, she got a large club stick and knife, and hastened to the place in which my mother was confined. She went into my mother's room with full intention to murder me with her knife and club, but as she was going to stick the knife into me, my grandmother happening to come in, caught the knife and saved my life. . . . My mother being half white, and my father a white man, I was at that time very white. Soon after I was six or seven years of age, my mother's old master died, that is, my father's wife's father. All his slaves had to be divided among the children. I have mentioned before of my father disposing of me; I am not sure whether he exchanged me and my mother for another slave or not, but think it very likely he did exchange me with one of his wife's brothers or sisters, because I remember when my mother's old master died, I was living with my father's wife's brother-in-law, whose name was Mr. Durham. My mother was drawn with the other slaves.

Roper recalled his sale to a slave trader, Mitchell.

My resembling my father so very much, and being whiter than the other slaves, caused me to be soon sold to what they call a negro trader, who took me to the southern states of America, several hundred miles from my mother. As well as I can recollect, I was then about six years old.

When Roper was thirteen years old he was bought by a sadistic slave master, Mr. Gooch of South Carolina. After many attempts, Roper succeeded in escaping from Gooch and making his way back to his mother in North Carolina.

> At last I got to my mother's house! My mother was at home; I asked her if she knew me. She said, No. Her master was having a house built just by, and as the men were digging a well, she supposed that I was one of the diggers. I told her I knew her very well, and thought that if she looked at me a little, she would know me; but this had no effect. I then asked her if she had any sons? She said, Yes; but none so large as me. I then waited a few minutes, and narrated some circumstances to her, attending my being sold into slavery, and how she grieved at my loss. Here the mother's feelings on that dire occasion, and which a mother only can have, rushed to her mind; she saw her own son before her, for whom she had so often wept. . . .

He was not only with his mother again, but also his stepfather and his brothers and sisters. He wanted to leave, to continue his escape to freedom, but his mother convinced him to stay. He remained for about a week, hiding in the woods during the day and sleeping in the cabin at night. One Sunday night, a group of angry men awakened him.

> [I] found my bed surrounded by twelve slave-holders with pistols in hand, who took me away (not allowing me to bid farewell to

those I loved so dearly) to the Red House,
where they confined me in a room the rest
of the night, and in the morning lodged me
in the jail of Caswell Court House.

He never saw his family again. A month
later Mr. Gooch retrieved him and punished him
severely.

They then took me home, flogged me, put
extra irons on my neck and feet, and put me
under the driver. . . . He did not flog me so
severely as before but continued it every
day. Among the instruments of torture
employed . . . is a machine for packing and
pressing cotton. By it he hung me up by the
hands . . . a horse moving round . . . and carrying it up and down. . . . At this time he
hung me up for a quarter of an hour. I was
carried up ten feet from the ground, when
Mr. Gooch asked me if I was tired. . . . He
then let me rest for five minutes, then carried me round again, after which he let me
down and put me into the box . . . and shut
me down in it for about ten minutes.

After the punishment, Roper stayed with Gooch for
several months before he tried to escape again.

Finally, Roper successfully escaped. He made
his way to Savannah, Georgia, where he managed
to board a ship and in six days, he arrived in New
York City. Afraid to stay in one place very long for
fear that slave catchers would apprehend him and
return him to slavery, he traveled throughout New
England. In Boston, the authorities attempted to
draft him into the military. The law clearly stated

that "no slave or colored person [could] perform this [military duty], but every other person in America of the age of twenty-one is called upon to perform military duty, once or twice in the year, or pay a fine." Nevertheless, Roper received the following document:

Mr. Moses Roper,

You being duly enrolled as a soldier in the company, under the command of Captain Benjamin Bradley, are hereby notified and ordered to appear at the Town House in Brookline, on Friday 28th instant, at 3 o'clock, P.M. for the purpose of filling the vacancy in said company occasioned by the promotion of Lieut. Nathaniel M. Weeks, and filling any other vacancy which may then and there occur in said company, and there wait further orders.

Unable to face the military authorities and reveal his true condition, Roper sailed for Liverpool, England, on November 11, 1835.

At the conclusion of his narrative Moses Roper writes of his feelings about the United States.

Whatever I may have experienced in America, at the hands of cruel task-masters, yet I am unwilling to speak in any but respectful terms of the land of my birth. It is far from my wish to attempt to degrade America in the eyes of Britons. I love her institutions in the free states, her zeal for Christ; I bear no enmity even to the slaveholders, but regret their delusions; many I am aware are deeply sensible of the fault, but some I regret to say are not, and I could wish to open their eyes to their sin; may the period come when God shall wipe off this deep stain from her constitution, and may America soon be indeed the land of the free.

Chapter three

Lewis Williamson
1841

∾

"The Story of Lewis Williamson. As related by Himself," published in *The Colored American* of November 13, 1841[3] shows that life was precarious even for free blacks.

Three miles below Gallapolis, I once possessed a farm of rich soil, that yielded seventy-five bushels to the acre.

I lived in comfort with my family around me and there I might have been living now, had not my prosperity raised the envy of a neighbor, whose land joined mine. He was heard to say (as I have since learned) that he would sell my children for money to pay for his farm.

He employed me (as I had some knowledge of the carpenter's trade) to assist in rebuilding a corn crib that had fallen five miles below. We could easily have done the work and returned home the same day had the other workmen been attentive to their business, but they loitered, and I with one or two others were sent to stay at his brothers; himself and the rest of the company were to spend the night at another house nearby. But far different was their intention. While they supposed me quietly resting, they were preparing a cruel dagger for my bosom.

At dead of night they entered my little habitation—rifled it of its most valuable contents, and dragged my wife and three small children from their beds. With savage brutality they were driven with naked feet over the frozen ground, two miles to the river, and thrown into a canoe. Two hundred and forty miles below, my wife was set on shore near midnight, in the woods. With a heart bursting with anguish, she sat till morning, when she found herself near Manchester, where she got on board of a steamboat and returned to her desolate home.

But to return to myself. I arose early. My rest had not been quiet. I thought of my family, from whom I never before had been unexpectedly absent, and something seemed to say, all is not well.

I set about finishing the work. The other workmen said it was too cold to work, and urged me to stop and take a dram [a drink of whiskey], but I refused.

When the business was accomplished, we set out for home. On the way, a neighbor came running to tell me the state in which he had seen my house. The horrible conviction flashed on my mind. I turned round to my employer, and said, "Did you get me away to sell my wife and children?"

He swore he knew nothing of it, but he looked like a monster to me, and if a weapon had been at hand, I fear I should have taken his life.

With all my strength, I pushed the canoe ashore, and ran to the neighbor's that came to tell me. Almost exhausted, I paused awhile to hear the melancholy tale. Sad was the sight of my lonely dwelling. Its disordered state, and the death-like silence, told, alas, too plainly, that the cruel spoiler had been there.

But I had no time to lose, and the thought that I might overtake and regain my dearest earthly treasures, spurred me on. I took passage in a steamboat for Louisville, [Kentucky], but could hear nothing of them. I then procured handbills, and had them distributed largely in every steamboat and place of note below, when it became necessary for me to return home. My wife was home before me.

[Time passes before the narrator resumes his search.]

On reaching Louisville the second time, my name was called by a Capt. Buckner, who had one of my handbills. I answered that was my name, though I might not be the person. I soon found that he had conveyed my children to Natchez, [a city on the Mississippi River] whither I pursued with all possible speed. On my arrival, I learned that they had been re-sold and taken three days before, no one, alas! knew whither.

I now wandered about in Mississippi, Alabama, Georgia, Tennessee, and Louisiana, in the forlorn hope of lighting upon them. [This covers a period of several years.] My sufferings were great. Though I found many ready to pity me, yet the anguish filled my heart. My children were slaves.

Almost despairing, I returned to Natchez. I then learned the name of the person in New Orleans on whom a draft was given by the second purchaser to the first. By writing to him, I found that he resided in Louisiana, about 80 miles from Natchez. I immediately went to his plantation, and saw my children, but did not make myself known to them or their master, for it might have prevented forever their return to liberty.

I returned home to procure one of my white neighbors for evidence. As compensation, I gave him my farm, besides a handsome suit of broadcloth, travelling expenses &c. When we arrived, the master was from home, and the mistress, who had heard of our coming, had sent the children 100 miles farther into the country.

But when the master came home, he sent for them. On the night in which they were expected, many people collected to witness the meeting. They had made a good fire, and some were sleeping, some were watching around it, while I was stationed at the quarter; my feelings were wrought up to the highest pitch. Hopes and fears conflicted. The messengers had already been gone longer that I was told at first they would probably be; and the whole might be but a plan to deceive me, and send them farther into bondage.

But about midnight I heard voices approaching and knew they were my children; I got up quickly, and reached the house before them. The people began to arouse, and said, "Wake up, Williamson." Ah! they thought a father could sleep—I had not slept for three nights.

I fell back from the light of the door, and saw them enter without speaking a word, but the tears ran down my cheeks to see their famished and miserable appearance. The man whom I had brought as witness kept his face from them for a time.

When he turned around and looked the boy (the eldest of the three) in the face, he rushed to him, exclaiming, "Oh Mr. Gibson, where's my father—my mother?"

I approached the door and said, "Why, Beck, are you here?"

My daughter dashed through the crowd, crying, "That's my father—oh father, where's mother?" and sunk in my arms.

After this, the owner said, "Old man, come in; these children are yours, and you must have them."

Thus joyfully ended my six years' search.

Chillicothe,
February 23, 1837

Frederick Douglass
1845

The *Narrative of the Life of Frederick Douglass, An American Slave*[4] was published in 1845. A revised and extended version entitled *My Bondage and My Freedom* was published in 1855. Toward the end of his remarkable life, Douglass published a third version of his autobiography entitled *Life and Times of Frederick Douglass* in 1881 and again in 1892. Douglass's autobiography is a classic work of American literature.

Douglass tells us he "was born in Tuckahoe, near Hillsborough, and about twelve miles from Easton, in Talbot County, Maryland. I have no accurate knowledge of my age ..." Douglass believed that the year of his birth was 1817, although it has been determined that he was born in 1818. Slaves were often kept ignorant of the date of their birth.

"My mother was named Harriet Bailey. . . . My father was a white man. He was admitted to be such by all I ever heard speak of my parentage."

His father is believed to have been his owner, Aaron Anthony, the manager of Colonel Lloyd's plantation on which Douglass and his family worked. For some time historians thought that Colonel Lloyd was Douglass's father.

His mother Harriet worked on a plantation twelve miles away from the Lloyd plantation, and the little boy was left in the care of his grandmother. "My mother and I were separated when I was an infant . . . ," Douglass says, and speculates on the reason children are separated from their mother by the slave owner. "For what this separation is done, I do not know, unless it be to hinder the development of the child's affection toward its mother, and to blunt and destroy the natural affection of the mother for the child.

"I never saw my mother to know her as such more than four or five times in my life. . . ." His mother died when he was seven years old.

When he was about five years old, he had to leave the shelter of his grandmother's cabin and go to live on the main plantation, the big farm owned by Colonel Lloyd. Douglass describes the plantation life in his account.

> The men and women slaves received, as their monthly allowance of food, eight pounds of pork, or its equivalent in fish, and one bushel of cornmeal. Their yearly clothing consisted of two coarse linen shirts, one pair of linen trousers, like the shirts, one jacket, one pair of trousers for winter, made of coarse negro cloth, one pair of stockings, and one pair of shoes; the whole of which could not have cost more than seven dollars. . . .

There were no beds given the slaves, unless one coarse blanket be considered such, and none but the men and women had these. . . . They find less difficultry from the want of beds than from the want of time to sleep; for when their day's work in the field is done, the most of them having their washing, mending, and cooking to do, . . . very many of their sleeping hours are consumed in preparing for the field the coming day; and when this is done, old and young, male and female, married and single, drop down side by side on one common bed—the cold, damp floor—each covering himself or herself with their miserable blankets . . .

Frederick, still too young for field work, was assigned chores about the house. The little boy often ran errands for Aaron Anthony's daughter, Mrs. Lucretia Auld, who seemed to like him. In 1826 Anthony retired, moved to a farm he owned, and took all his slaves with him, except little Frederick. Frederick was sent to the brother of Captain Anthony's son-in-law, Hugh Auld, who lived in Baltimore.

Frederick, who was eight years old, was taken aback by his new owner's wife for she was unlike any other white women he had met. The behavior he had learned in his father's house did not serve him well in her presence.

The crouching servility usually so accept-able a quality in a slave did not answer when manifested toward her. . . . She did not deem it impudent or unmannerly for a slave to look her in the face. . . .

Very soon after I went to live with Mr. and Mrs. Auld, she very kindly commenced to teach me the ABC. After I had learned this, she assisted me in learning to spell words of three or four letters. Just at this point of my progress, Mr. Auld found out what was going on and at once forbade Mrs. Auld to instruct me further, telling her . . . that it was unlawful, as well as unsafe, to teach a slave to read. To use his own words, . . . "If you give a nigger an inch, he will take an ell. A nigger should know nothing but to obey his master—to do as he is told to do. Learning would spoil the best nigger in the world. . . . It would forever unfit him to be a slave. He would at once become unmanageable, and of no value to his master. As to himself, . . . It would make him discontented and unhappy."

From that moment, I understood the pathway from slavery to freedom. . . . Though conscious of the difficulty of learning without a teacher, I set out with high hope, and a fixed purpose, at whatever cost of trouble, to learn how to read.

Douglass now set about developing strategies for learning alone.

The plan which I adopted, and the one by which I was most sucessful, was that of making friends of all the little white boys whom I met in the street. As many of these as I could, I converted into teachers. With their kindly aid, obtained at different times and in different place, I finally succeeded in learning to read. When I was sent on errands, I always took my book with me, and by doing one part of my errand quickly, I found time to get a lesson before my return. I used also to carry bread with me, enough of which was always in the house, and to which I was always welcome; for I was much better off in this regard than many of the poor white children in our neighborhood. This bread I used to bestow upon the hungry little urchins, who, in return, would give me the more valuable gift of knowledge.

I was now about twelve years old and the thought of being a slave for life began to bear heavily on my heart.

Douglass got hold of a book entitled *The Columbian Orator,* a collection of famous speeches. The more he read, the more he learned about slavery and the more he hated slavery and the enslavers. In time he came to feel that "learning to read had been a curse rather than a blessing."

By this time, Frederick resolved to run away. "I was too young to think of doing so immediately; besides I wished to learn how to write as I might have occasion to write my own passes." He used similar stratagems to learn to write.

. . . When I met any boy who I knew could write, I would tell him I could write as well as he. The next word would be, "I don't believe you. Let me see you try it." I would then make the letters which I had been so fortunate as to learn, and ask him to beat that. In this way I got a good many lessons in writing, which it is quite possible I should never have gotten in any other way. During this time, my copy-book was the board fence, brick wall, and pavement; my pen and ink was a lump of chalk. With these I learned mainly how to write. I then commenced and continued copying the italics in Webster's Spelling Book, until I could make them all without looking on the book.

In March, 1832, due to a falling out between Hugh Auld and his brother Thomas, Frederick had to leave Baltimore and return to Thomas Auld in the country.

Thomas Auld decided that city life had greatly affected Douglass. He sent Douglass to a slave breaker, Mr. Edward Covey. On January 1, 1833 Douglass left Mr. Auld and went to live with Covey, where for the first time in his life he was a field hand. He was hired out to Covey for one year. "During the first six months of that year, scarce a week passed without his whipping me."

"You have seen how a man was made a slave; you shall see how a slave was made a man." One day while working, Douglass became sick. Mr. Covey, in an attempt to force Douglass to return to work, kicked him.

He then gave me a savage kick in the side, and told me to get up. I tried to do so, but fell back in the attempt. He gave me another kick, and again told me to rise. I again tried, and succeeded in gaining my feet . . . I again staggered and fell. Mr. Covey took up

[a] hickory slat . . . and with it gave me a
heavy blow upon the head, making a large
wound, and the blood ran freely . . . .

Douglass decided that he did not have to tolerate
such abuse. He would return to his owner, Mr.
Auld, and report to him what had happened. He
succeeded in getting a considerable distance into
the woods before Mr. Covey discovered him.
However, Douglass eluded Mr. Covey and made his
way to Mr. Auld, who justified Covey's behavior and
told Douglass that he must return. On his way
back to Covey, Douglass ran into another slave,
Sandy Jenkins. Jenkins alsotold him that he must
return, but before going

I must go with him into another part of the
woods, where there was a certain root,
which, if I would take some of it with me,
carrying it always on my right side, would
render it impossible for Mr. Covey or any
other white man to whip me. He said he had
carried it for years; and since he had done
so, he had never received a blow, and never
expected to while he carried it.

Douglass at first rejected the idea, but soon gave in
to Sandy Jenkins's conviction in the power of the
root.
Douglass returned and all went well until he
went into the stables, where Mr. Covey attacked
him. He resolved to fight back. "My resistance was
so entirely unexpected, that Covey seemed taken all
aback." He and Mr. Covey tussled for nearly two
hours. "Covey at length let me go, puffing and blow-
ing at a great rate, saying that if I had not resisted,

he would not have whipped me so much. The truth was, that he had not whipped me at all." For the last six months of Douglass's stay with Covey, he never tried to whip him again. "This battle with Mr. Covey was the turning-point in my career as a slave. It rekindled the few expiring embers of freedom, and revived within me a sense of my own manhood."

Covey could have had the constable take Douglass to the whipping post, where he would have been flogged for raising his hand to a white man. Douglass speculates that Covey did not do this because he "enjoyed the most unbounded reputation for being a first-rate overseer and negro-breaker. . . . That reputation was at stake; and had he sent me—a boy about sixteen years old—to the public whipping post, his reputation would have been lost; so, to save his reputation, he suffered me to go unpunished.

After his time with Covey, Douglass was hired out to Mr. William Freeland.

". . . [I]n a very little while after I went there, I succeeded in creating in [Freeland's slaves] a strong desire to learn how to read. . . . They very soon mustered up some old spelling-books, and nothing would do but that I must keep a Sabbath school. I agreed to do so, and accordingly devoted my Sundays to teaching these my loved fellow-slaves how to read. . . .

I had at one time over forty scholars, and those of the right sort, ardently desiring to learn. They were of all ages, though mostly men and women. I look back to those Sundays with an amount of pleasure not to be expressed. They were great days to my

soul. The work of instructing my dear fellow-slaves was the sweetest engagement
with which I was ever blessed. We loved
each other, and to leave them at the close of
the Sabbath was a severe cross indeed.

For the ease with which I passed the year, I
was, however, somewhat indebted to the
society of my fellow-slaves. They were noble
souls; they not only possessed loving hearts,
but brave ones. We were linked and inter-
linked with each other. I loved them with a
love stronger than any thing I have experienced since. It is sometimes said that we
slaves do not love and confide in each other.
In answer to this assertion, I can say, I
never loved any or confided in any people
more than my fellow-slaves, and especially
those with whom I lived at Mr. Freeland's. I
believe we would have died for each other.

In 1835, while living with Freeland, Douglass
"began to want to live upon free land as well as
with Freeland." He began to plan his escape. He
and four other slaves, Henry Harris, John Harris,
Henry Bailey, and Charles Roberts, were part of
the plan. Douglass wrote the passes:

This is to certify that I, the undersigned,
have given the bearer, my servant, full
liberty to go to Baltimore, and spend the
Easter holidays. Written with mine own
hand, &c., 1835.

WILLIAM HAMILTON,
Near St. Michael's, in
Talbot County, Maryland

Unfortunately, the group was betrayed, apprehended, and sent to the jail. Douglass expected Mr. Auld to sell him into the Deep South. "But, from some cause or other, he did not send me to Alabama, but concluded to send me back to Baltimore . . . to learn a trade. . . . My Master sent me away because there existed against me a very great prejudice in the community, and he feared I might be killed."

In Baltimore, Douglass was hired out to a shipbuilder, Mr. Gardner; however, because of the prejudice of the white workers Douglass was physically forced to leave after eight months.

Until a very little while after I went there, white and black ship-carpenters worked side by side, and no one seemed to see any impropriety in it. All hands seemed to be very well satisfied. Many of the black carpenters were freemen. Things seemed to be going on very well. All at once, the white carpenters knocked off, and said they would not work with free colored workmen. Their reason for this, as alleged, was that if free colored carpenters were encouraged, they would soon take the trade into their own hands, and poor white men would be thrown out of employment. They therefore felt called upon at once to put a stop to it. . . . My fellow apprentices very soon began to feel it degrading to them to work with me. They began to put on airs, and talk about the "niggers" taking the country, saying we all ought to be killed.

Mr. Hugh Auld then hired him out to another ship-builder where within one year he was receiving the highest wages given to the most experienced calkers.

> I now come to that part of my life during which I planned, and finally succeeded in making, my escape from slavery. But before narrating any of the peculiar circumstances, I deem it proper to make known my intention not to state all the facts connected with the transaction. . . .Were I to give a minute statement of all the facts, it is not only possible, but quite probable, that others would thereby be involved in the most embarrassing difficulties. Secondly, such a statement would most undoubtedly induce greater vigilance on the part of slaveholders . . . which would . . . be the means of guarding a door whereby some dear brother bondman might escape his galling chains.

(In later versions of his autobiography, Douglass does detail the facts of his escape.)

By 1838 Douglass was becoming quite restless. He could see no reason for giving his pay to his owner every week. Eventually he convinced Hugh Auld that he should have the privilege of hiring his own time. "I was to pay him three dollars at the end of each week; find myself in calking tools, and in board and clothing."

Douglass worked in this manner from May until August, when his owner refused to allow Douglass to continue hiring his time because of his failure to pay Hugh Auld on time one week. Douglass decided to make a second attempt at escape. Meanwhile, he "masked" his plans by becoming a model slave, turning over large sums of money, between eight and nine dollars, to his owner. In return Hugh Auld gave Douglass twenty-five cents, a very large amount for a slave-owner to give a slave.

". . . on the third day of September 1838, I left my chains and succeeded in reaching New York."

> I had been in New York but a few days, when Mr. Ruggles sought me out, and very kindly took me to his boarding-house at the corner of Church and Lispenard Streets. Mr. Ruggles was then very deeply engaged in the memorable Darg case, as well as attending to a number of other fugitive slaves, devising ways and means for their successful escape; and though watched and hemmed in on almost every side, he seemed to be more than a match for his enemies.

Mr. Ruggles thought it was unsafe for Douglass to remain in Baltimore, and advised him to go to New Bedford, where Douglass could get work in his trade as a ship's caulker.

His intended wife, Anna, who was a free woman, joined him from Baltimore. Three days after his arrival in New Bedford, Massachusetts, Douglass found a job. "There was no Master Hugh standing ready, the moment I earned the money, to rob me of it. . . . I was at work for myself and newly married wife." His new job was not caulking, however, because again there was much prejudice among the white caulkers who refused to work with blacks.

The paper (*The Liberator*) came, and I read it from week to week with such feelings as it would be quite idle for me to attempt to describe. The paper became my meat and my drink. My soul was set all on fire.

I took right hold of the cause (anti-slavery reform). I could do but little but what I could I did with a joyful heart, and never felt happier than when in an anti-slavery meeting. . . . While attending an anti-slavery convention at Nantucket, on the 11th of August, 1841, I felt strongly moved to speak. . . . The truth was, I felt myself a slave, and the idea of speaking to white people weighed me down. I spoke but a few moments, when I felt a degree of freedom, and said what I desired with considerable ease. From that time until now, I have been engaged in pleading the cause of my brethren—with what success, and with what devotion, I leave those acquainted with my labors to decide.

William Lloyd Garrison, editor of the *Liberator*, was present at the anti-slavery convention when Frederick Douglass spoke. Douglass was hired by the Massachusetts Anti-Slavery Society to tour the Northern states giving speeches on abolitionism. Some people, hearing this brilliant and eloquent lecturer, doubted that he could ever have been a slave. As a result, many abolitionists urged Douglass to write his own narrative.

After the Narrative was published, Douglass established a newspaper for black abolitionists, the *North Star*, later *Frederick Douglass's News-*

paper. Douglass went on to be one of the outstanding leaders of the Abolitionist movement, and was an adviser to President Lincoln during the Civil War. After the Civil War he held many posts, including that of U.S. Ambassador to the Republic of Haiti.

William Wells Brown
1847

The *Narrative of William Wells Brown, Fugitive Slave*[5] was published in 1847 in Boston by the Anti-Slavery Society. A well-known abolitionist, Brown helped escaped slaves reach Canada. He authored *Clotelle, or The President's Daughter*, which was published in London in 1853 and in the United States in 1864 and is considered the first novel by an African-American.

William Wells Brown was born in Lexington, Kentucky, one of seven children. As was customary in the circumstances of slavery, no two of the seven children had the same father. "My father's name, as I learned from my mother, was George Higgins. He was a white man, a relative of my master, and connected with some of the first families in Kentucky". Brown grew up on the plantation where he worked as a house servant, "a situation preferable to that of a field hand, as I was better fed, better clothed, and not obliged to rise at the ringing of the bell . . ." His mother, Elizabeth, on the other hand, was a field hand.

Brown witnessed dreadful scenes on the plantation. One morning his mother was ten or fifteen minutes late getting to the field. For this offense the overseer began whipping her. "She cried, Oh! pray—Oh! pray—Oh! pray"—these were generally the words of slaves, when imploring mercy at the hands of their oppresssors. Brown jumped out of bed. He stood at the door listening to the crack of the whip and the screams of his mother. Unable to help her, he wept.

Brown recalls another incident of brutality that he witnessed while living on the plantation. Randall, a slave, had refused a whipping. The overseer, Cook, ignored the unmanageable slave for about a week. Finally, he again asked Randall to allow himself to be tied, but Randall still refused. The overseer and his companions then attempted to tie Randall for his whipping, but the slave resisted. The overseer drew his pistol and shot him.

> The others rushed upon him with their clubs, and beat him over the head and face, until they succeeded in tying him. He was then taken to the barn, and tied to a beam. Cook [the overseer] gave him over one hundred lashes with a heavy cowhide, had him washed with salt and water, and left him tied during the day. The next day he was untied, and taken to a blacksmith's shop, and had a ball and chain attached to his leg. He was compelled to labor in the field, and perform the same amount of work that the other hands did. When his master returned home, he was much pleased to find that Randall had been subdued in his absence.

When Brown's owner moved to the city of St. Louis, Missouri, he took Brown and his mother with him. In St. Louis, Brown was hired out to Major Freeland, who kept a public house. Major Freeland was particularly brutal. ". . . When he wished to chastise one [of his servants], he would tie them up in the smoke-house, and whip them; after which, he would cause a fire to be made of tobacco stems, and smoke them. This he called '*Virginia play*.' " Brown complained to his owner about his treatment, but the owner cared nothing about it as long as he received the money for his labor.

After Brown had lived with Major Freeland for five or six months, he ran away. He was caught in the woods by slave-hunting dogs and sent to the St. Louis jail. Major Freeland took him home from jail and flogged him and then sent his son, Robert, a young man eighteen or twenty years of age to flog him also. Afterward, Brown was well smoked.

Brown was then sent to work for the Reverend Elijah P. Lovejoy, the publisher and editor of a St. Louis newspaper. "Mr. Lovejoy was a very good man, and decidedly the best master that I had ever had. I am chiefly indebted to him, and to my employment in the printing office, for what little learning I obtained while in slavery." Unfortunately, Brown did not remain long with Lovejoy. Elijah Lovejoy, an abolitionist, was run out of St. Louis for protesting in his newspaper the lynching of a black man. In 1837 Lovejoy was murdered for his abolitionist agitation by a local mob in Alton, Illinois.

Shortly after his stay with Lovejoy, Brown was hired out as a waiter on the Mississippi River steamboat *Enterprize*.

... In passing from place to place, and seeing new faces every day, and knowing that
they could go where they pleased, I soon
became unhappy, and several times thought
of leaving the boat at some landing place,
and trying to make my escape to Canada,
which I had heard much about as a place
where the slave might live free, and be pro-
tected.

Whenever such thoughts arose, Brown thought of
his enslaved mother. He could not bear to be free
while she was still a slave. When Brown confided
this to his sister she urged him to take the chance
to escape to freedom. "I beseech you not to let us
hinder you. If we cannot get our liberty, we do not
wish to be the means of keeping you from a land of
freedom."

At one of its ports the boat took on board a
drove of slaves bound for the New Orleans market.
Among the slaves was a very beautiful young
woman, "apparently about twenty years of age, perfectly white, with straight light hair and blue eyes."
Although Brown was unable to learn the history of
the woman, this chance meeting was possibly the
basis of his novel, *Clotelle*, about the slave daughter of a United States president.

On this trip, Brown learned many details of the
slave trade. One of his tasks was to prepare the
older slaves for market, by shaving off their
whiskers and plucking out the gray hairs. If there
were too many gray hairs to be plucked, he black-
ened the hair so that the elderly slaves looked
much younger.

Next Brown's owner hired him out to Mr.
Walker, a slave trader who operated between St.

Louis and New Orleans. In St. Charles, Missouri, Walker purchased a slave woman with a four- or five-week-old child in her arms. Soon after leaving St. Charles, the baby became very irritable, crying throughout the day. Mr. Walker complained and told the mother to stop the child's noise or he would. The baby, however, continued to cry. "He [Walker] took the child by one arm, as you would a cat by the leg, walked into the house, and said to the lady, 'Madam, I will make you a present of this little nigger; it keeps such a noise that I can't bear it.'" The mother, when she saw her child was to be left, ran to Walker, begging him to let her have her child, but Walker refused.

After a year with Walker, Brown escaped. He slipped away in winter and walked through the countryside at night, following the north star. While walking north, he reflected on his life in slavery.

His original name had been William; however, because his owner's nephew was also named William, his mother had been ordered to change Brown's surname to Sanford. As a free man, Brown decided to retake the name of William and drop Sanford.

> It is sometimes common in the south for slaves to take the name of their masters. Some have a legitimate right to do so. But I always detested the idea of being called by the name of either of my masters .... So I was not only hunting for my liberty, but also hunting for a name. . . .

After four nights his food ran out. By the fifth or sixth day of his travels, his thin summer clothes were covered with ice. Fortunately a Quaker, Wells Brown, discovered him, saved him from dying of the cold and sheltered him in his own home.

In gratitude for saving his life, Brown took the name of his benefactor.

After two weeks the escaped slave discovered that he was about sixty miles from Dayton, Ohio. From Dayton he could go to Cleveland on Lake Erie and from Cleveland he could enter Canada, his final destination.

> An American citizen was fleeing from a Democratic, Republican, Christian government, to receive protection under the monarchy of Great Britain. While the people of the United States boast of their freedom, they at the same time keep three millions of their own citizens in chains; and no law . . . can protect me from the hands of the slaveholder!

> Soon after coming North, I subscribed to the *Liberator*, edited by that champion of freedom William Lloyd Garrison. I labored a season to promote the temperance cause among the colored people, but for the last three years, have been pleading for the victims of American slavery.
>
> WILLIAM WELLS BROWN.
> Boston, Mass., June, 1847.

After his own escape, Brown led other escaping slaves into Canada by way of Cleveland, Ohio.

Henry Bibb
1849

The *Narrative of the Life and Adventures of Henry Bibb, An American Slave*[6] was published in 1849 in New York.

Henry Bibb was born May 1815 of a slave mother, in Shelby County, Kentucky, the property of David White, Esquire.

> My mother was known by the name of Mildred Jackson. She is the mother of seven slaves only, all being sons, of whom I am the eldest. She was also fortunate or unfortunate, as to have some of what is called the slaveholding blood flowing in her veins. I know not how much; but not enough to prevent her children though fathered by slaveholders, from being bought and sold in the slave markets of the South.

Like many slaves, it was almost impossible for Bibb "to give a correct account of his male parentage." Bibb's mother had informed him that his father was James Bibb, "of the present Bibb family of Kentucky; but I have no personal knowledge of him at all. . . ."

When he was eight or ten years old he was taken from his mother and hired out to work for various persons. All the money he earned was used to pay for the education of Harriet White, his owner's daughter. Because of his constant work, the only thing he was able to learn was the art of running away. "I made a regular business of it, and never gave it up, until I had broken the bands of slavery. . . ."

When he was about eighteen years old he fell in love with Malinda, a mulatta slave on a nearby plantation. Malinda moved in the highest circle of slaves and free people. Bibb notes,

> The distinction among slaves is as marked as the classes of society are in any aristocratic community, some refusing to associate with others whom they deem beneath them in point of character, color, or the superior importance of their respective masters.

At first, Bibb had no intention of courting or marrying Malinda. "But in spite of myself, before I was aware of it, I was deeply in love; and what made this passion so effectual and almost irresistible, I became satisfied that it was reciprocal."

Now that he had fallen in love, he began wondering if he wanted to bring a child into slavery.

> But oh! That I had only then been enabled to have seen as I do now, or to have read the following slave code, which is but a

stereotyped law of American slavery. It would have saved me I think from having to lament that I was a husband and am the father of slaves who are still left to linger out their days in hopeless bondage. The laws of Kentucky, my native state, with Maryland and Virginia, which are said to be the mildest slave States in the Union, noted for their humanity, Christianity and democracy, declare that "Any slave, for rambling in the night, or riding horseback without leave, or running away, may be punished by whipping, cropping and branding in cheek, or otherwise, not rendering him unfit for labor. Any slave convicted of petty larceny, murder, or wilfully burning of dwelling houses, may be sentenced to have his right hand cut off; to be hanged in the usual manner, or the head severed from the body, the body divided into four quarters, and head and quarters stuck up in the most public place in the county, where such act was committed.

Before proposing marriage, he declared to Malinda,

"I never will give my heart nor hand to any girl in marriage, until I first know her sentiment upon the all-important subjects of Religion and Liberty, no matter how well I might love her, nor how great the sacrifice in carrying out these God-given principles. And I here pledge myself from this course never to be shaken while a single pulsation of my heart shall continue to throb for Liberty."

Malinda shared his beliefs. They discussed the subject of marriage and entered into a conditional contract to marry in one year if they did not change their minds. They pledged their love and honor. "There was nothing that was more binding upon slaves than this. . .

> . . . for marriage among American slaves, is disregarded by the laws of this country. It is counted a mere temporary matter; it is a union which may be continued or broken off, with or without the consent of a slaveholder, whether he is a priest or a libertine.

> There is no legal marriage among the slaves of the South. . . . And be it known to the disgrace of our country that every slaveholder, who is the keeper of a number of slaves of both sexes, is also the keeper of a house or houses of ill-fame. Licentious white men, can and do enter at night or day the lodging places of slaves; break up the bonds of affection in families; destroy all their domestic and social union for life; and the laws of the country afford them no protection.

Henry's mother opposed the marriage because she thought that he was too young and marrying would involve him in trouble and difficulty. His future mother-in-law opposed the marriage because she wanted her daughter to marry a slave "who belonged to a very rich man living near by, and who was well known to be the son of his master." Henry's owner opposed the marriage because "he feared my taking off from his farm some of the fruits of my own labor for Malinda to eat, in the shape of pigs, chickens, or turkeys, and would count it not robbery." Other men also opposed this marriage because they wanted Malinda for themselves.

However, Malinda's owner was in favor of the marriage. "When I went to ask his permission to marry Malinda, his answer was in the affirmative with but one condition, which I consider to be too vulgar to be written in this book."

They married during the Christmas holidays. "Malinda was to me an affectionate wife. She was with me in the darkest hours of adversity. She was with me in sorrow, and joy, in fasting and feasting, in trial and persecution, in sickness and health, in sunshine and in shade."

Some months after their marriage, Bibb's owner sold his farm to move to Missouri. Finally, after Henry's repeated requests, he sold Henry to his brother, who had a farm within seven miles of Malinda's owner. Henry was so defiant and insubordinate with this new owner that he was sold to William Gatewood, Malinda's owner. Though he now lived on the same farm as Malinda, and his new owner was no more cruel than his former owner, Henry was unhappy.

> . . . To live where I must be eye witness to her insults, scourgings and abuses, such as are common to be inflicted upon slaves, was more than I could bear. If my wife must be exposed to the insults and licentious passions of wicked slave-drivers and overseers; if she must bear the stripes of the lash laid on by an unmerciful tyrant; if this is to be done with impunity, which is frequently done by slaveholders and their abettors, Heaven forbid that I should be compelled to witness the sight.

A few months after Henry went to live on Gatewood's farm, Malinda gave birth to a baby girl, Mary Frances, who was cherished by her parents. Soon after Mary Frances's birth, Malinda returned to work in the fields. While Malinda was working, the baby was left with Mrs. Gatewood, the owner's wife, who physically abused her. Henry laments, "She is bone of my bone, and flesh of my flesh; poor unfortunate child. She was the first and shall be the last slave that ever I will father for chains and slavery on this earth."

Unable to tolerate the abuse of his wife and child, Henry escaped to Canada. and then returned to rescue his wife and child and bring them North to Canada. He was caught by the slave hunters, but soon escaped from them. Because Malinda was watched day and night, the couple decided not to run away then. Malinda had him concealed in the house of a friend while they fearfully waited for an opportunity to escape to Canada.

> They well knew that my little family was the only object of attraction that ever had or ever would induce me to come back and risk my liberty over the threshold of slavery— therefore this point was well guarded by the watch dogs of slavery, and I was compelled again to forsake my wife for a season, or surrender, which was suicidal to the cause of freedom. . . .

He finally determined that escape for the three together was impossible, and that their only chance lay in making their escapes separately. On his departure, Malinda promised that within two months she would meet him at a predetermined place in Ohio.

After I had waited three months for the arrival of Malinda, and she came not, it caused me to be one of the most unhappy fugitives that ever left the South. I had waited eight or nine months without hearing from my family. I felt it to be my duty, as a husband and father, to make one more effort. I felt as if I could not give them up to be sacrificed on the "bloody altar of slavery." I felt as if love, duty, humanity and justice, required that I should go back, putting my trust in the God of Liberty for success.

Henry returned South a second time to try to rescue Malinda and Mary Frances. But he was caught and jailed. Malinda's owner, who had been trying without success to seduce her, tied her to a post and lashed her two days in succession. To torment her further, the owner also told Malinda that he had sold Mary Frances. Finally, he "drove Malinda before him to the workhouse swearing by his Maker that she would submit to him or die."

Several weeks later the family was reunited on a coffle, a train of slaves fastened together, bound for sale in New Orleans. In New Orleans, a Baptist church deacon and cotton planter, Francis Whitfield, bought them as a family. While they were owned by the deacon, Malinda became very ill. Henry writes, "While she was sick, we lost our second child, and I was compelled to dig my own child's grave and bury it myself without even a box to put it in."

Henry did not give up his attempts to escape. After being punished with five hundred lashes for going to a prayer meeting, Henry decided to run away again, but fear of being caught sent him back to the plantation. Together Malinda and Henry tried to escape, but this plan was also thwarted. Because of his repeated attempts to escape, the deacon sold him to a group of gamblers, but he refused to sell Malinda and Mary Frances. This time, December 1840, was the last occasion when Henry saw his wife and child.

His gambler-owners wandered into Indian territory where a wealthy half-Indian of the Cherokee Nation bought him. Henry was grateful for this change.

> First, I thought I should stand a better chance to get away from an Indian than from a white man. Second, he wanted me only for a kind of a body servant to wait on him—and in this case I knew that I should fare better than I should in the field. And my owners also told me that it would be an easy place to get away from.

Henry says the Cherokee slave owner "was the most reasonable and humane slaveholder that I have ever belonged to."

> The Indians allow their slaves enough to eat and wear. They have no overseers to whip nor drive them. . . . So far as religious instruction is concerned, they have it on terms of equality, the bond and the free; they have no respect of persons, they have neither slave laws nor negro pews. Neither do they separate husbands and wives, nor parents and children. All things considered, if I must be a slave, I had far rather be a slave to an Indian than to a white man from the experience I have had with both.

After the death of his Cherokee owner, Henry escaped.

In the winter of 1845 Henry again returned South, seeking to rescue Malinda and Mary Frances. He learned that his "wife was living in a state of adultery with her master, and had been for the last three years. . . . The child . . . was still with her. Whitfield, their former owner, had sold her to this man for the above purposes at a high price." Sorrowfully, he returned North. In June 1848, he married Miss Mary E. Miles of Boston.

> She is to me what a poor slave's wife can never be to her husband while in the condition of a slave; for she can not be true to her husband contrary to the will of her master. She can neither be pure nor virtuous, contrary to the will of her master. She dare not refuse to be reduced to a state of adultery at the will of her master; from the fact that the slaveholding law, customs and teachings are against the poor slaves.

Henry Bibb includes in his narrative his answer to a letter from his former master, W. H. Gatewood.

> You may perhaps think hard of us for running away from slavery, but as to myself, I have but one apology to make, which is this: I have only to regret that I did not start at an earlier period. . . . To be compelled to stand by and see you whip and slash my wife without mercy when I could afford her no protection, not even by offering myself to suffer the lash in her place, was more than I felt it to be the duty of a slave husband to

endure, while the way was open to Canada. My infant child was also frequently flogged by Mrs. Gatewood, for crying, until its skin was bruised literally purple. This kind of treatment was what drove me from home and family to seek a better home for them.

In 1851, two years after publication of his narrative, Henry Bibb began the Refugees' Home Colony in Canada which purchased 1,300 acres in Canada for settlement by ex-slaves.

Henry Box Brown
1851

This *Narrative of the Life of Henry Box Brown,* 1851[7] shows the ingenuity and the incredible lengths to which enslaved Africans would go for freedom. In his escape Brown was aided by members of the underground railroad, in particular William Still, who was a black man and the secretary of The Vigilance Committee. Still was known as a "brakeman" on the underground railroad and his Philadelphia home was a busy "station." After the war, William Still wrote an account of these activities entitled *Underground Railroad.*

Brown was born fifty-five miles from the city of Richmond, Virginia in 1815.

> I entered the world a slave—in the midst of a country whose most honoured writings declare that all men have a right to liberty—but had imprinted upon my body no mark which could be made to signify that my destiny was to be that of a bondsman.

As he grew up on the plantation, his mother introduced him to Christianity and proper slave behavior. While he was young, his principle employment was waiting upon his owner and the owner's family. When he grew older, one of his tasks was carrying grain to the mill several times a year. Once, he and his brother happened upon another group of slaves.

> They were dressed with shirts made of coarse bagging, such as coffee-sacks are made from, and some kind of light substance for pantaloons, and no other clothing whatever. They had on no shoes, hats, vests, or coats, and when my brother asked them why they spoke of our being dressed with those articles of clothing, they said they had "never seen negroes dressed in that way before."

In addition to their scant dress, the slaves were also very hungry. Brown and his brother shared their food with them. The two young men asked many questions, including whether the men in the group had any wives.

> The one who gave us the information said they had wives, but were obliged to marry on their own plantation. Master would not allow them to go away from home to marry, consequently he said they were all related to each other, and master made them marry, whether related or not.

Henry's brother then asked if they had sisters.

> . . . He said he could not tell them from the rest, *they were all his sisters;* and here let

me state, what is well known by many people, that no such thing as real marriage is allowed to exist among the slaves. Talk of marriage under such a system!

Henry comments on the relationship of slaveowners with slave women and how this relationship affected the black family.

The slave's wife is his, only at the will of her master, who may violate her chastity with impunity. It is my candid opinion that one of the strongest motives which operate upon the slaveholders, and induce them to retain their iron grasp upon the unfortunate slave, is because it gives them such unlimited control in this respect over the female slaves. The greater part of slaveholders are licentious men, and the most respectable and the kindest of masters keep some of their slaves as mistresses. It is for their pecuniary interest to do so in several respects. Their progeny is so many dollars and cents in their pockets, instead of being a bill of expense to them as would be the case if their slaves were free; and mulatto slaves command a higher price than dark colored ones; but it is too horrid a subject to describe. Suffice it to say, that no slave has the least certainty of being able to retain his wife or her husband a single hour; so that the slave is placed under strong inducements not to form a union of love, for he knows not how soon the chords wound around his heart would be snapped asunder by the hand of the brutal slave-dealer.

Eventually, Henry was sent to Richmond, Virginia, to work in a tobacco factory, leaving his family behind. While he was in Virginia, Nat Turner's rebellion occurred. In 1831 in an attempt to free themselves from slavery, Nat Turner and an armed group of slaves attacked the white people of the plantations in Southampton, Virginia. Before they were killed or captured, the rebel slaves had killed more than fifty white people. Armed slave uprisings were the greatest fear of the slave masters, and following the Nat Turner rebellion, repression in the South was intensified. In his narrative Henry describes how some of the slaves suspected of involvement in the insurrection were tortured.

> Great numbers of the slaves were locked in the prison, and many were "half hung," as it was termed; that is, they were suspended to some limb of a tree, with a rope about their necks, so adjusted as not to quite strangle them, and then they were pelted by men and boys with rotten eggs. This half-hanging is a refined species of cruelty, peculiar to slavery. . . .

Henry soon met a young woman from another plantation whom he wished to marry. Henry's owner talked to her owner, Mr. Lee, and they were allowed to marry, and Mr. Lee promised not to sell Henry's wife away from the plantation. Contrary to his promise, however, Mr. Lee sold Henry's wife to a very cruel woman, and when Henry returned home from work one day, he found his wife and children gone. When Henry complained to his owner, he was told that he could get another wife.

> Marriage was not a thing of personal conve-
> nience with me, to be cast aside as a worth-
> less garment whenever the slaveholder's
> will requested it; but it was a sacred institu-
> tion binding upon me as long as God who
> had "joined us together, refrained from
> untying the nuptial knot."

Despondent over the sale of his wife and children,
Henry decided to run away.

> The first thing that occurred to me, after
> the cruel separation of my wife and chil-
> dren from me, and I had recovered my sens-
> es, so as to know how to act, was thoughts
> of freeing myself from slavery's iron yoke.
> I had suffered enough under its heavy
> weight. . . .

After much thought and prayer, Henry received a
message.

> "Go and get a box, and put yourself in it." I
> pondered the words over in my mind. "Get a
> box?" thought I. "What can this mean?" But
> I was not disobedient unto the heavenly
> vision, and I determined to put into practice
> this direction, as I considered it, from my
> heavenly Father. I went to the depot, and
> there noticed the size of the largest boxes,
> which commonly were sent by the cars, and
> returned with their dimensions.

Henry asked a carpenter to make him a box which
measured 3 feet 1 inch by 2 feet 6 inches by 2 feet.
Members of the underground railroad assisted
Henry. A "friend" in Richmond had arranged for the

box to be sent to an address in Philadelphia. And so Henry's journey began.

On the morning of the twenty-ninth day of March 1849, I went into the box—having previously bored three gimlet holes opposite my face, for air, and provided myself with a bladder of water, should I feel getting faint. I took the gimlet[1] also with me, in order that I might bore more holes if I found I had not sufficient air. Being thus equipped for the battle of liberty, my friends nailed down the lid and had me conveyed to the Express Office, which was about a mile distant from the place where I was packed. I had no sooner arrived at the office that I was turned heels up, while some person nailed something on the lid of the box. I was then put upon a waggon and driven off to the depot, then the man who drove the waggon tumbled me roughly into the baggage car, where, however, I happened to fall on my right side.

The next place we arrived at was Potomac Creek, where the baggage had to be removed from cars, to be put on board the steamer; where I was again placed with my head down, and in this dreadful position had to remain nearly an hour and a half, which, from the sufferings I had thus to endure, seemed like an age to me. I felt my eyes swelling as if they would burst from their sockets; and the veins on my temples were dreadfully distended with pressure of

[1] A small tool with a screw-like tip for boring holes.

blood upon my head. In this position I attempted to lift my hand to my face but I had no power to move it; I felt a cold sweat coming over me which seemed to be a warning that death was about to terminate my earthly miseries, but as I feared even that less than slavery, I resolved to submit to the will of God, and, under the influence of that impression, I lifted up my soul in prayer to God, who alone was able to deliver me. My cry was soon heard, for I could hear a man saying to another, that he had travelled a long way and had been standing there two hours, and he would like to get something to sit down; so perceiving my box, standing on end, he threw it down and then two sat upon it. I was relieved from a state of agony which may be more easily imagined than described. I could now listen to the men talking, and heard one of them asking the other what he supposed the box contained; his companion replied he guessed it was "THE MAIL." I, too, thought it was a mail but not such a mail as he supposed it to be.

Henry's next stop was Washington, where he overheard a person saying that there was no room for the box. It would have to stay in the depot and be sent through on the luggage train.

... But the Lord had not quite forsaken me, for in answer to my earnest prayer He so ordered affairs that I should not be left behind; and I now heard a man say that the box had come with the express, and it must be sent on. I was then tumbled into the car with my head downward again, but the car had not proceeded far before, more luggage having to be taken in, my box got shifted about and so happened to turn upon its right side; and in this position I remained till I got to Philadelphia.

In Philadelphia the box, with Henry in it, sat in the depot until seven o'clock, when a contact from the underground railroad arrived and asked for the box. The box was then placed in a wagon and delivered to a station of the underground railroad as his "friend" in Richmond had arranged.

A number of persons soon collected round the box after it was taken into the house, but as I did not know what was going on I kept myself quiet. I heard a man say, "Let us rap upon the box and see if he is alive"; and immediately a rap ensued and a voice said, tremblingly, "Is all right within?" to which I replied— "All right." The joy of the friends was very great; when they heard that I was alive they soon managed to break open the box, and then came my resurrection from the grave of slavery. I rose a freeman, but I was too weak, by reason of my long confinement in that box, to be able to stand; so I immediately swooned away.

Josiah Henson
1851

One of the most popular novels of the nineteenth century was Harriet Beecher Stowe's *Uncle Tom's Cabin or Life among the Lowly* (1852). According to the legend, when Abraham Lincoln met Mrs. Stowe, he is supposed to have said, "So this is the little lady who wrote the book that started the big war." Mrs. Stowe allegedly based some of the adventures of her title character, Uncle Tom, on the life of ex-slave Josiah Henson, which were relayed in his autobiography, *Truth Is Stranger Than Fiction.*[8]

Josiah Henson was born June 15, 1789, near Port Tobacco in Charles County, Maryland, on a farm owned by Francis Newman. One of his earliest memories was of the appearance one day of his father with his head bloody and his back mutilated. Josiah did not know what had happened, but he picked up part of the story from slave gossip.

Henson's father had heard his wife screaming and he immediately went to help her.

> The overseer, who was a rough, coarse man,
> without the least consideration for the phys-
> ical, mental or moral rights of the human
> beings under his charge, had brutally
> assaulted my mother.

Henson's father would have killed the overseer had
it not been for his wife's intervention. The overseer
promised that nothing would be said about the
attack on Henson's mother. Of course, the promise
was not kept.

The laws of the slave states were specific; no
slave must strike a white man. The penalty was
very clearly stated as "one hundred lashes on the
bare back, and to have the right ear nailed to the
whipping-post, and then severed from the body."

Knowing that this was the penalty, Henson's
father hid in the woods, only venturing to the cabin
for food. At length, his supplies were cut off and he
was starved out. Hunger compelled him to turn
himself in.

After receiving one hundred lashes, "his head
was then thrust against the post; and his right ear
fastened to it with a tack; a swift pass of a knife,
and the bleeding member was left sticking to the
place." The punishment was carried out in front of
an audience of slaves and whites. At the end, a
cheer came from the crowd.

> . . . And the exclamation, "That's what he's
> got for striking a white man." A few said,
> "it's a damned shame"; but the majority
> regarded it as but a proper tribute to their
> offended majesty.

Before the incident Henson's father had been a
cheerful, lighthearted person. After the punish-

ment, he changed. He became sullen and morose. No threat, not even the risk of being sold further South, could return him to his former disposition. Finally, the owner sold him to someone in Alabama. Henson heard nothing of his father since.

Eventually Henson's owner died. His property, including his slaves, was sold. At the auction Henson's mother was mercilessly kicked for asking her new owner to buy her son too, so that they could be together. The man refused, and Henson was bought by another. Henson soon fell sick and seemed likely to die. The slaveholder who had purchased Henson offered to sell him for a small sum, so that the mother and son could be together.

The new master was "coarse, vulgar, and cruel," and "brutality was the order of the day." Henson spent more than thirty years as the slave of this man.

When Henson was about twenty-two years old, he married a woman from a neighboring plantation whom he met at a religious meeting. "She bore me twelve children, seven of whom still survive and have been the comfort of my declining years."

In April 1825 his owner sent Henson to Davis County, Kentucky to live with his brother, who owned a large plantation. Henson remained there three years. His owner's brother had given Henson a position as superintendent of the plantation.

In Kentucky, Henson had the opportunity of attending camp meetings.

> . . . I became better acquainted with those religious feelings which are deeply implanted in the breast of every human being, and learned by practice how best to arouse them, and keep them excited, how to stir up the callous and indifferent, and, in general,

to produce some good religious impressions
on the ignorant and thoughtless community
by which I was surrounded.

For three years from 1825 to 1828, Henson took
advantage of all opportunities to learn more about
God and the Bible and then was ordained a minister in the Methodist church.

In time, Henson arranged with his owner to
buy his freedom for 450 dollars. Henson had raised
the money by preaching and had paid his owner
350 dollars in cash and given him a note for the
remaining hundred dollars. His owner convinced
Henson that he should not travel with his free
papers. Instead his owner assured Jenson that he
would send his free papers in a letter to his brother
in Maryland. Cunningly, his owner had raised the
price of Henson's freedom to one thousand dollars.
Now Henson's balance was 650 dollars.

The owner did not like looking at Henson,
because the sight of Henson reminded him daily of
his wickedness. Henson's owner took him to New
Orleans to be sold without informing him of the
real purpose of the trip. In New Orleans, the owner
became very ill with a stomach disorder and
Henson nursed him back to health. Instead of selling Henson the owner returned to Kentucky with
him. Now the only thoughts that occupied Henson
concerned how and when to escape.

But, alas! I had a wife and four dear children;
how should I provide for them? Abandon
them I could not, no, not even for the blessed
boon of freedom. They, too, must go. They,
too, must share with me the life of liberty.

Once his plans were formulated, he told his wife.

> She was overwhelmed with terror. With a
> woman's instinct she clung to hearth and
> home. She knew nothing of the wide world
> beyond, and her imagination peopled it with
> unseen horrors. We should die in the wilder-
> ness—we should be hunted down with
> bloodhounds—we should be brought back
> and whipped to death. . . . She was a poor,
> ignorant, unreasoning slave woman.

He finally convinced her by telling her that "though
it would be cruel trial for me to part with her, I
would nevertheless do it, and take all the children
with me except the youngest. . . ." She reluctantly
agreed to attempt the escape with him.

As superintendent, Henson rode to different
parts of the plantation every day. His cabin was
near the boat landing, and all his family was there
except his oldest son, who was the houseboy for the
owner. Henson planned to leave on the weekend
because it would give him several days before he
would be missed.

> Some time previously I had got my wife to
> make me a large knapsack, big enough to
> hold the two smallest children; and I had
> arranged it that she should lead the second
> boy, while the oldest was stout enough to go
> by himself and to help me carry the neces-
> sary food. I used to pack the little ones on
> my back, of an evening, trot around the
> cabin with them . . . to accustom . . . myself
> to the task before us.

At length the eventful night came. I went up to the house to ask leave to take Tom home with me, that he might have his clothes mended. No objection was made, and I bade Master Amos "good night" for the last time. It was about the middle of September, and by nine o'clock in the evening all was ready. It was a dark, moonless night, and we got into the little skiff, in which I had induced a fellow slave to set us across the river. It was an anxious moment. We sat still as death.

A month later on October 28, 1830, the family reached Canada. In Canada, Henson supported his family with preaching and day labor. He also traveled as an antislavery lecturer. On one of his trips to Andover, Massachusetts, he met Harriet Beecher Stowe. She asked him to tell her the story of his life and his tale became the inspiration for parts of *Uncle Tom's Cabin.*

James Smith
1852

After the Fugitive Slave Law was signed by President Millard Fillmore on September 18, 1850, many runaway slaves in the North went to Canada, where they were beyond the reach of the U.S. law and the slave catchers. In Canada the ex-slaves established communities which often had their own abolitionist newspapers. The following narrative, "The Lost Is Found", was serialized monthly in a Canadian abolitionist newspaper of Sandwich, Canada West, *Voice of the Fugitive,* in 1852.[9] The narrative is reprinted as it appeared in the newspaper.

"THE LOST IS FOUND" NO. 1
VOICE OF THE FUGITIVE,
JANUARY 15, 1852

James Smith, a refugee from slavery, has met with the unspeakable joy of finding his wife in Canada, after an absence of 17 years.

He gives the following interesting sketch of his experience, escape, &c. About sixteen years ago, Mr. Smith was held in the state of Virginia by one Wm. Wright, who was a hard master. While he was the slave of this man, he became a convert to the Christian religion, and made an application to the Baptist church, one Sabbath Day to be admitted into the church and the ordinances of baptism; but the minister refused to have anything to do with him until he could see Mr. Wright (his master), who was a member of the same church, about it.

After the preacher had seen his master, who consented that he should be baptized if he should be found worthy after being examined, he informed James that on the next Sabbath he should be examined as a candidate for baptism. On the day appointed, he was accordingly examined. Many questions were asked him to which he answered and gave general satisfaction, but before he was discharged, his master had one or two question to ask, viz.: "Do you feel as if you loved your master better that you ever did before, and as if you could do more work and do it better? Do you feel willing to bear correction when it is given you, like a good and faithful servant, without fretting, murmuring, or running away as has heretofore been your prac-tice? If so, it is an evidence that you are a good boy, and you may be baptized." He was finally received into the church and baptized.

Not long after this, he felt loudly called upon to go out and labor for the salvation of souls among the slave population with whom he was identified. At this conduct his master was much displeased, and strove to prevent him from the exercise of what the slave considered to be his duty to God and his brethren on the Sabbath Day. He was sometimes kept tied all day Sundays while the other slaves were allowed to go just where they pleased on that day. At other times he was flogged until his blood would drip down to his feet, and yet he would not give up laboring whenever he could get an opportunity, on the Sabbath Day, for the conversion of souls. God was pleased to bless his labors and many were led to embrace the Saviour under his preaching.

At length his master sold him to a slave trader, who separated him from his family and carried him to the state of Georgia. His parting words to his wife were that if they proved faithful to God, He would bring them together again in a more free land than Virginia.

(To be continued)

"THE LOST IS FOUND" NO. 2
VOICE OF THE FUGITIVE
THURSDAY, FEBRUARY 25, 1852

The reader will remember that this is a combination of the sad story of James Smith, the fugitive who after the lapse of 17 years had the good fortune to find his bereaved wife in Canada, whom he had left a slave in the state of Virginia. Mr. Smith who is a clergyman of the Baptist faith and order, it will be remembered, was held and worked for many long years in the state of Virginia, by a member of the same denomination, who separated him from his wife and little ones and sold him to a slave trader in Georgia.

After he was sold to the soul-driver, Mr. White, his former master in explaining his character to this new master said that there "was but one fault to this boy." He was trustworthy, faithful, hard to work &c., but he would run about at nights and on

Sundays trying to preach the gospel amongst the slave population, which had a tendency to divert their attention from their work, and made them dissatisfied also, and that he had frequently flogged him with a rough hide until his back was literally bathed with blood, and yet he'd slip off and do the same thing over again. "Ah," said the new master, "I can soon break him of that practice when I have had him staked down with his face to the ground, and his back striped and checked with the lash,—with salt and red pepper well rubbed in the gashes, he will give up and forget his religion."

Just at this time poor Smith was ordered to get ready his little bundle of clothing to start with the chain gang, which was then standing in the road, under the command of a savage driver. On entering his humble cabin for the last time, to gather up his few garments of old clothing, and then to take leave of his affectionate wife and two little ones, he says, "Oh, at that moment it seemed as if my poor heart would break with grief." After pressing his little ones to his breast, he kneeled and commended them to the God of Heaven; but before these religious exercises were concluded he was driven from his knees by the stern voice of the driver, who brought the handcuffs and locked them about his wrists.

Under this most afflicting trial his wife seemed to bear up with Christian fortitude, striving to console her husband by pledging herself to meet him in a better world than this. But, oh, when the word of command was given for the coffle gang to move off it was more than this wife and slave mother could bear without sobbing. When the parting hand was given, the poor woman burst into tears and wept aloud. This solemn and heart rending scene can never be described.

From there they were driven to Georgia where

poor Smith was placed under an overseer and a cruel driver, on a cotton plantation where there were not less than 300 hands. His quarters were in a small hovel wherein lodged ten persons including himself, and the rules were strictly against their holding any religious meetings. At length Smith ventured to violate this rule, so far as singing and praying was concerned, in his lodging place. Other slaves soon became interested in praying and the news was reported to the overseer by the driver, who was ordered to take Smith, and give him one hundred lashes for violating the plantation law.

When he was brought to the gin house to be flogged, he was asked by the driver why he prayed in the cabin, and if he was let to pass that time without being punished if he would ever pray again! To which his reply was that he could never pledge himself to refrain from praying, though his life should be [ended]. For this expression he was most unmercifully "bruised" and "mangled." The next night he ran away, but was overtaken the day following, with dogs. He was brought back, repunished and put under guard both night and day.

(To be continued)

"THE LOST IS FOUND" NO. 3
VOICE OF THE FUGITIVE
THURSDAY, MARCH 11, 1852

By day poor Smith was not only strictly watched while at his labor, by the slave driver, who was himself a black man, but had a heavy chain and clog of iron to drag after him as he toiled in the field. All night he was chained up to a heavy block of wood under the driver's care who was charged not to allow him to sing or pray. The poor man yet clung to the helm of prayer. After he supposed that all was asleep in the cabin but himself, which was generally after midnight, he would pour out his sufferings before the great deliverer and "king of all the earth." But he was overheard one night by the driver, whose heart was so much affected at hearing Smith praying for him and the overseer, that he came and took off the chain and wept on account of the punishment which he had been compelled to inflict upon a Christian man for worshipping his creator. After taking the continued prayers and forgiveness of Smith for the cruel punishment which he had received at his hand, he told him to go just where he pleased, and he should never try to recapture him again. Smith thanked him for his kindness, and started that night for the state of Virginia, where he hoped to find his wife.

By concealing himself by day and traveling by night for six or eight weeks, he succeeded in making his way back to where he had been separated from his little family. It was at the dead hour of night when he found his way back to the plantation from whence he had been driven in a chain gang from friends and family to a far distant land.

With all the anxiety of a bereaved husband and father he approached the supposed habitation of his own family with fear and trembling. He did not dare to rap at the door, fearing that there might be persons within who would betray him; but he ventured to open the door softly for himself as it had no fastening. He stepped over several persons who were lying asleep on the floor, and moved gently towards one corner of the room where his wife used to sleep; but before he had reached that corner of the cabin, there was a white man, who sprang out of another bed between him and the door with a large knife and pistol in hand swearing by his maker that if he attempted to move another step, that he would shoot him dead on the spot. He was lying with a slave girl and was not asleep when Smith entered the hut. By this time all the slaves in the room were up, and ordered by this white man, who was their overseer, to strike up a light and "lay hold of this strange negro." Not recognizing him in the dark, they asked for his name, which he refused to give. While they were kindling up a light, his determination was to make a rush for the door, even if he should fall a victim to death in the attempt. But reason remonstrated against it; he saw the glittering knife, and the thought of being murdered and strangled in his own blood like a dumb beast in the room where he hoped to have a happy greeting with his little family, from whom he had been absent for more than eighteen months, deterred him from making the attempt. While he was thus trembling between hope and fear one of the slaves recognized him and said, "This is Jim, who master sold to the nigger trader. He has come back after Fan, his wife, but master has sold her too." At this moment the white man ordered them again to lay hold of him or knock him down, which order was immediately obeyed.

(To be continued)

"THE LOST IS FOUND" NO. 4
VOICE OF THE FUGITIVE
THURSDAY, APRIL 2, 1852

The reader will remember that this is the resumed story of James Smith, the fugitive.

The writer commenced giving this narrative some time back. In consequence of the absence of Mr. Smith, it was left unfinished. We have already said in No. 2 that after the lapse of seventeen years, this fugitive, who was sold and separated from his wife in the state of Virginia, had the good fortune, after years of unrequited labor, suffering, and perilous adventures to find her in Canada West. We now call attention to the difficulty into which Smith had fallen with the overseer who had taken lodging with a female slave in the slaves' cabin. The order given by the overseer was to "lay hold of him or to knock him down," which order was immediately obeyed by an able-bodied black man, who struck Smith on the back part of his head with a heavy club, which brought him senseless to the floor.

The next morning about 9 o'clock when he awoke from this half dead state, bathed in blood, he found himself bound with strong cords, lying in a horse cart (like a slaughtered hog) driven by the overseer himself, who was conducting him to the cold dungeon of the Richmond jail wherein he was kept for several months.

While there he learned from another slave that his wife for whom he had suffered almost death itself, had been sold by her master to a trader, who carried her to the state of Kentucky.

At length his master came after him with the spirit of a demon. After having him stripped and most unmercifully flogged, a hot iron was applied to his quivering flesh on one side of his face and back of his neck which left stamped in letters of flesh and blood, the initials of his master's name.

A few days after this punishment, he was sold at public auction to Wm. Graham, with whom he lived about three years, during which time he resolved to run away to Canada, where he had learned from an Irishman, that every colored man who ran away from slavery and went there was made free by the laws of Great Britain.

This [agreement] he [made] to the slave who

agreed to come with him to Canada. Their masters worked them both hard and fed them very scantily, and had it not been for the raccoons, opossums, and other small game which Mr. Smith and his friend used to catch in the woods after night, by the aid of a good hunting dog, they must have suffered many times almost unto starvation. But Smith had taken the precaution to train up a good hunting dog which by the by will be seen to have proved truer to his master that his supposed human friend, for on the night that they were to start for this country they had agreed to meet together at a certain place where Smith did arrive at the appointed hour. But instead of finding his professed friend there, he found a company of armed white men, who had been apprised of the scheme by Smith's companion, for the sum of one dollar in money and a half gallon of whiskey.

When Smith started from his humble cabin that night, in pursuit of his long subverted rights, his faithful hunting dog moved off prancing before him. Smith tried to drive him back, but this proved to be all in vain. As he drew near the spot where he and his friend were to meet, the dog commenced to growl and bark and got before his master as though he was trying to prevent him from advancing to the place where these highwaymen were lying [sic] concealed to capture the poor man. He supposed that the dog was only barking at his professed friend, until his enemies had surrounded and taken him as criminal condemned for the love of liberty. The struggle was desperate for a while between the white men against the slave and his devoted dog before they were conquered.

After Smith was knocked down and completely overcome, his dog, which had bit two of the party, reluctantly fled away, or followed at a great distance. Doubtless fearing that he should be killed for the active part which he had taken in defence of his master, he still bore his testimony against them by raising an awful howling when he heard the piteous cries of his master, who was stripped, tied up and flogged by the bloodthirsty party who captured him. They then took him home and called up the man who had betrayed him and who was there made to repeat the whole plot before Smith. They then and there paid the traitor a half gallon of whiskey and one dollar in money for his base treachery to Smith.

The whole crowd drank whiskey so freely that night that they became stupid and careless about Smith. They made him drink several times, after which he made them believe that he was almost dead drunk. Several of them said that he was so drunk that he would not be able to stir before the next morning, so they retired and left Jim lying on the kitchen floor, as they supposed, drunk and asleep.

About one hour afterward when he supposed that all was asleep he bid a final adieu to the abodes of slavery and resumed his journey for Canada. He had not proceeded far from the house before he was again greeted by his devoted hunting dog, which seemed to be filled with joy at the release of his master. He endeavored to drive him back, but did not succeed, The dog determined to follow him. When he had travelled about fifteen miles on his way, he discovered the dawn of daylight breaking upon him, which forced him to seek a place of concealment during the day. He crouched by the side of an old mossy log with his dog close by his side. The dog seemed to be quite restless and to be filled with fearful apprehensions. Every stick that cracked or leaf that rattled seemed to arouse his senses to watchful care so that Smith thought that he had better kill him, lest some one should be passing through the woods and the dog bark at them which would betray his whereabouts. Having with him the rope with which the drunken party had left him tied the night before, he fastened it about the dog's neck and led him to a small tree where the poor fellow was to be executed. The dog looked up at his master while he was tying the rope with all the intelligence of a human being and the devotion of an undaunted friend. Making no resistance whatever, he appeared to be willing to lay down his life for the liberation of his master.

This singular conduct on the part of the dog led Jim to pause and ask himself the question, whether it would be right in the sight of God for him to take the life of that dog, which had proved so true to him in the hour of danger? Just as he was reflecting over the matter he heard the yelling of a pack of blood hounds coming on his trail, so he immediately released his dog and started on a run but did not proceed far before they were overtaken by the dogs.

To be finished in our next issue, if the writer is not necessarily called away.

(To be continued)

"THE LOST IS FOUND" NO. 5
VOICE OF THE FUGITIVE
THURSDAY, APRIL 22, 1852

In No.4 we left Smith and his hunting dog, surrounded and kept at bay for a short time, by the blood hounds; but there being only three of them in number, they were soon killed or compelled to retreat. Smith had prepared himself with a heavy club for self-defence, and at the approach of the blood-hounds, his dog seized one of them by the neck and held him fast, which resulted in bringing the dogs all into a blood fight, during which engagement Smith succeeded in killing two of the blood-hounds with his club and the other was glad to escape with his life, which was in great danger. This victorious struggle, by the aid of the faithful hunting dog, endeared him to his master stronger than ever; for without his aid Smith must have been taken back into slavery. From thence they proceeded north to the Virginia and Ohio line, which occupied several nights.

They travelled by night and kept concealed by day until they reached the above (Ohio) river with no other guide than the north star. In wandering up and down the stream to find a conveyance to cross in, he saw a large steamboat passing down the stream which confirmed him in the belief that this was the Ohio River, having heard much about the steamboats running that river. He at length found a skiff tied to a tree on the shore, in which he ferried himself across, leaving his dog behind, but he had not proceeded far before he discovered that the dog had plunged into the stream and was close behind the boat, and succeeded in crossing even before his master.

The next morning he saw an old gentleman in the woods chopping some poles to whom he ventured to speak, and in whom he found a friend and an abolitionist. This friend took him and his dog with him home and after giving them some refreshments sent them on to another friend about thirty miles distant, who gave him employment for five years and while there his valuable dog died. He was engaged in agricultural pursuits and preached occasionally among the people of color in that vicinity.

From thence he came to Huron County, Ohio,

where he purchased a small farm and lived on it about seven years, having given up all hopes of ever seeing his wife again; but in the fall of 1850, after the enactment of the Fugitive Slave Bill, the news came to him that a warrant was out for him, and that if he did not flee away to Canada, he would be taken as a slave. On the strength of this report, at a very great sacrifice, he sold his property and came to Canada.

While travelling about among his fugitive brethren and occasionally telling where he was originally from, he found a man who told him he knew a woman in Canada who was from near Richmond, Virginia, who had once belonged to a man there by the name of Wm. Wright and that he sold her, &c. This, of course, aroused Mr. Smith's curiosity to see the woman; so he went the next day to where he had been told that she lived. As he approached the house he saw a female whom he thought resembled "Fanny," his long bereft wife; and, as he approached her with trembling lest he might be mistaken, he offered his hand and ventured to call her by her former name to which she answered with astonishment. At this moment her eyes sparkled and flashed like strokes of lightning upon his furrowed cheeks and wrinkled brow and with uplifted hands and joyful heart she exclaimed from the depths of her soul, "Oh! is this my beloved husband who I never again expected to see?" To this appeal there was a glorious response on the part of the husband; they embraced each other in the bonds of Christian love and wept aloud for joy and glorified God with their bodies and spirits which are his for his great mercy in bringing them together again on this earth; and they are now living happily together on the Queen's "Free Soil."

Their children have all been scattered and sold

apart so that the mother knows not where they are; she ran away from her master in Kentucky in 1847, and has been in Canada about three years. Thus we must end the Narrative of Mr. and Mrs. Smith which might be lengthened but our limits will not permit.

"A Short and True Story of a Fugitive" 1855

This short account, published in 1855 in an abolitionist newspaper *The Provincial Freeman* in Canada, describes from the perspective of the runaway the aid given to a slave by abolitionists.[10]

A poor slave lived in the far South. He felt it was hard to be at the will of a master, to be bought and sold and whipped and driven, as if a beast of the land. He, by some means, had heard that far to the North, there is a land of freedom called Canada. He determined to be free or die in the effort to gain what seemed to him dearer than life. In the dark night he started upon his long and dangerous journey. In the day time he hid himself in dark recesses and unfrequented places; and again he travelled at night wandering . . . when clouds covered the starry heavens, and when the sky was clear, the North Star was his guide.

He had nothing to eat but the little he could gather at night by the way. Often he was hungry and faint. Often he sighed and slept alone, driven from the sympathy of all his fellow beings. His heart leaped at the sound of the rustling leaves as if the footsteps of the pursuers were heard.

Many worrisome days and nights passed again—at length he crossed the Ohio River into Clermont County, state of Ohio. His clothes were worn out and his shoes were without bottoms and he had no food to eat. Pressing want forced him to venture again upon the dwellings of men. He offered himself to a farmer as a day laborer. The farmer and his family had prejudices against the poor man because he was black. This was very wrong; the poor man could not help being black. The farmer hired him because he was in need of a laborer. In a few days the farmer and his family forgot all about the color of the poor runaway slave and became very much attached to him. He ventured to tell them that he was on his way to Canada, and how far he had come, and that he needed shoes and clothes and money to enable him to reach the land of safety.

The farmer took his horse and rode to town, a few miles distant, in which an anti-slavery society had been formed, and said to the abolitionists, "There is a runaway slave at my home. He has come a great distance, he needs clothes and shoes and money." . . . These good but persecuted people bought him clothes and provided money for the expenses and gave all to the poor fugitive slave. His heart melted in him. He wept like a child! . . . for he was so overjoyed he could not speak. Here in a strange land he found white people not enemies but brothers and sisters, ready to aid him in his trials and wants. It had never before entered his mind that there were such white people on earth!

How happy those people must have been in

relieving and making happy a poor colored brother. How "blessed is he that considers the poor!" Heavenly father will bless those that will relieve the oppressed and show mercy to the afflicted, but He will be offended at those who despise the poor black man and He will punish them unless they repent and seek forgiveness through the merits of the Savior.

Solomon Northup
1853

Twelve Years a Slave. The Narrative of Solomon Northup, a Citizen of New York, Kidnapped in Washington City in 1841, and Rescued in 1853, from a Cotton Plantation near the Red River in Louisiana was published in 1853.[11]

Slave history is filled with stories of blacks and some whites who were kidnaped and sold into slavery. After the passage of the fugitive slave law in 1850, slave hunters from the South were able to come to the North to search for and capture blacks suspected of having fled from their owners to the free states. As a result of the new law many free blacks were able to be kidnapped and brought South under the pretext that they were escaped slaves. For free blacks, escaped slaves and abolitionists, the kidnapping of men and women in the North was an additional cause of outrage that needed to be publicized. . . . Solomon Northup is an excellent example of a narrative written by a free Black who was sold into slavery.

Solomon Northup was born to free parents in Minerva, Essex County, New York in July 1808. His father, Mintus Northup, had been born a slave but he was manumitted (given his freedom) at his owner's death. Mintus Northup was a hardworking, thrifty man who accumulated enough property to be able to vote.

On December 25, 1829, Solomon married Anne Hampton, a woman living in the vicinity.

> From the time of my marriage to this day the love I have borne in my wife has been sincere and unabated, and only those who have felt the flowing tenderness a father cherishes for his offspring can appreciate my affection for the beloved children which have since been born to us. This much I deem appropriate and necessary to say, in order that those who read these pages may comprehend the poignancy of those sufferings I have been doomed to bear.

From this marriage the couple had three children: Elizabeth, Margaret, and Alonzo. In March 1835 the family moved to Saratoga Springs, New York.

One day two men approached Solomon, offering him a job driving a team south for one dollar a day. Northup accepted, and on April 7, 1841, the three arrived in Washington City (D.C.). After their arrival, Northup became ill with a stomach disorder and one of the men brought him some medicine to ease the pain. This is the last thing Northup remembered before waking up handcuffed and chained to the floor of a slave pen operated by a Mr. Williams. Northup asked why he was in chains and Williams said it was because he was a slave.

> I asserted, loudly and boldly, that I was a free man—a resident of Saratoga, where I had a wife and children, who were also free and that my name was Northup. I complained bitterly of the strange treatment I had received, and threatened, upon my liberation, to have satisfaction for the wrong.

Burch, the slave trader, called him a liar, had him stripped and whipped with a paddle and cat-o'-nine tails.

> The paddle, as it is termed in slave-beating parlance, or at least the one with which I first became acquainted, and of which I now speak, was a piece of hard-wood board, eighteen or twenty inches long, moulded to the shape of an old-fashioned pudding stick or ordinary oar. The flattened portion, which was about the size in circumference of two open hands, was bored with a small auger in numerous places. The cat was a large rope of many strands—the strands unraveled, and a knot tied at the extremity of each.

Burch promised Northup that he would kill him if he ever mentioned to anyone that he was a free man.

Northup was held in the slave pen for about two weeks and then the slave traders took him by boat to Richmond, Virginia. In Richmond, the slaves were unloaded by Theophilus Freeman, another slave trader, who loaded them onto another boat that sailed for New Orleans.

At the slave market in New Orleans, Mr. Ford of Rapide Parish, Louisiana bought Solomon Northup. Solomon worked as a carpenter for Ford for about a year but Ford soon had financial problems and had to sell Northup. A Mr. Tibault bought him, but sold him in a short time to Edwin Epps of Bayou Beouf, Louisiana.

Northup spent nine agonizing years on Epp's plantation. Despite the atrocities committed against him and the other slaves, Northup eventually became overseer. In one passage of the narrative, Northup describes the Christmas holidays for the slaves.

> The only respite from constant labor the slave has through the whole year is during the Christmas holidays. . . . It is the only time to which they look forward with any interest or pleasure. They are glad when night comes not only because it brings them a few hours' repose but because it brings them one day nearer Christmas. It is hailed with delight by the old and the young. . . . It is the time of feasting and frolicking and fiddling—the carnival season with the children of bondage. They are the only days when they are allowed a little restricted liberty, and heartily indeed do they enjoy it.

While falsely enslaved, Northup had repeatedly tried to get word to his friends and family in the North, but with no success. Eventually he managed to get a letter to the North. When his friends received the letter, they immediately petitioned the governor of New York to secure his release. Finally, he was freed and the following year he entered the home of his wife and their children.

As I entered their comfortable cottage, Margaret was the first that met me. She did not recognize me. When I left her, she was but seven years old, a little prattling girl, playing with her toys. Now she was grown to womanhood—was married, with a bright-eyed boy standing by her side. Not forgetful of his enslaved, unfortunate grand-father, she had named the child Solomon Northup Staunton. When told who I was, she was overcome with emotion, and unable to speak. Presently Elizabeth entered the room, and Anne came running from the hotel, having been informed of my arrival. They embraced me, and with tears flowing down their cheeks, hung upon my neck. But I draw a veil over a scene which can better be imagined than described.

Chapter twelve

William and Ellen Craft
1860

〜

Running a Thousand Miles for Freedom, The Story of William and Ellen Craft[12] describes the escape from slavery of a husband and wife. Many narratives deal with the escape of the man who then returns for his family. This narrative, one of the few about a husband-and-wife team, was widely read just before the Civil War.

William and Ellen Craft were born in different towns in the slave state of Georgia.

It is true, our condition as slaves was not by any means the worst; but the mere idea that we were held as chattels, and deprived of all legal rights—the thought that we had to give up our hard earnings to a tyrant, to enable him to live in idleness and luxury— the thought that we could not call the bones and sinews that God gave us our own; but above all, the fact that another man had the power to tear from our cradle the new-born babe and sell it in the shambles like a brute, and then scourge us if we dared to lift a finger to save it from such a fate, haunted us for years.

William and Ellen planned their escape. Ellen's owner was also her father and her mother was one of his slave women. William writes, "Notwithstanding my wife being of African extraction on her mother's side, she is almost white. . . ." Ellen's resemblance to members of her owner's family had caused the owner's wife such great annoyance, that his wife had given Ellen, when she was eleven years old, to her daughter as a wedding present. Craft decided to use his wife's coloring as the key to their plan of escape.

It may be remembered that slavery in America is not at all confined to persons of any particular complexion; there are a very large number of slaves as white as any one. . . .

The two had realized the near impossibility of escaping from slavery in Georgia and then traveling for many miles across other slave states before reaching freedom. Therefore, they resolved to marry and adapt as much as possible to the system of slavery, while being constantly on guard for any chance to escape.

At last in December 1848, they came up with a plan. Knowing that slave holders could take their slaves to any part of the country, it occurred to Craft that "as my wife was nearly white, I might get her to disguise herself as an invalid gentleman, and assume to be my master, while I could attend as his slave." He suggested the plan to his wife, who at first refused because of the difficulty of the plan. However, she also considered her circumstances as a slave. "She saw that the laws under which we lived did not recognize her to be a woman, but mere chattel to be bought and sold, or otherwise dealt with as her owner might see fit." Ellen finally approved the plan.

William began to purchase the items needed for the disguise.

> It is unlawful in Georgia for a white man to trade with slaves without the master's consent. But notwithstanding this, many persons will sell a slave any article that he can get the money to buy. Not that they sympathize with the slave, but merely because his testimony is not admitted in court against a free white person.

With little difficulty William purchased everything he needed except the trousers, which Ellen made.

When they had everything together, they asked the owner to allow them to be away for a few days. In this way their absence would not be immediately noticed. Ellen obtained a pass from her owner. The cabinetmaker with whom William worked gave him a similar paper. The Crafts assumed that the passes said what they hoped they said since neither could read or write.

They were ready to leave when they realized that it was the custom to sign guest books at hotels. On the verge of despair, Ellen came up with a plan. She said, "I think I can make a poultice[2] and

[2]A soft heated mass of bread or white clay applied to an inflamed or sore area of skin

bind up my right hand in a sling, and with propriety ask the officers to register my name for me." Ellen also reasoned that her beardless face would expose her. ". . . She decided to make another poultice, and put it in a white handkerchief to be worn under the chin, up to the cheeks, and to tie over the head. This nearly hid the expression of the countenance, as well as the beardless chin."

Since Ellen would be passing as a white man and spending time in the company of other men, she felt that she needed something to cover her eyes. William purchased a pair of green spectacles for her. Just before the time for them to leave arrived, William cut off her hair and she dressed in her disguise.

Ellen did not want to participate in the plan, but she knew that it was not customary in the South for women to travel with male servants. There was no other choice than for her to pass as a white man. "My wife's being muffled in the poultices furnished a plausible excuse for avoiding general conversation, of which most Yankee travellers are passionately fond."

When they were finally ready to leave their slave cabin, fear overwhelmed them. "We had to take our lives, as it were, in our hands, and contest every inch of the thousand miles of slave territory over which we had to pass. . . ."

The Crafts took different routes to the railroad station. William took the quickest route and "my master (as I will now call my wife) took the longer way round, and only arrived there with the bulk of the passengers." William bought two tickets for Savannah, Georgia.

Just before the train pulled out of the station, William peeked through the window to see Ellen.

There, to his great astonishment, was the cabinet-maker with whom he had worked. William fully expected to be caught and dragged out at any moment; however, the cabinetmaker looked into the carriage but did not recognize Ellen.

> I have since heard that the cabinetmaker had a presentiment that we were about to "make tracks for parts unknown"; but, not seeing me, his suspicions vanished, until he received the startling intelligence that we had arrived safely in a free state.

From Savannah they took a train to Fredericks-burg, Virginia, where they took a steamer to Washington, D.C. They had left their slave cabin on the 21st of December 1848 and arrived in Baltimore Saturday evening, the 24th. In Baltimore, which was the last major slave port at which they had to stop, the authorities always watched carefully for any blacks who might be try-ing to escape into Pennsylvania, a free state.

A train official stopped them in the Baltimore railroad station. He told William that he should get off the train because "the train will soon be leaving. It is against my rules to let any man take a slave past here, unless he can satisfy them in the office that he has a right to take him along." The couple went to the railroad office, where the "principal man" was waiting for them. The "principal man" informed them,

> If we should suffer any gentleman to take a slave past here into Philadelphia; and should the gentleman with whom the slave might be travelling turn out not to be his

rightful owner; and should the proper master come and prove that his slave escaped
on our road, we shall have him to pay for it;
and, therefore, we cannot let any slave pass
here without receiving security to show, and
to satisfy us, that it is all right.

A bell rang announcing the departure of the train
and the railroad official, unsure of what to do,
finally decided that they could take the train. "As
he is not well, it is pity to stop him here. We will let
him go." The Crafts travelled to Philadelphia where
Ellen collapsed from nervous exhaustion.

As it was not safe for them in Philadelphia,
they continued on to Boston where William found
employment as a cabinetmaker and Ellen worked
as a seamstress. Their happiness did not last long
for in 1850 Congress passed the Fugitive Slave Bill
which required. . .

Under heavy penalties, that the inhabi-
tants of the free states should not only
refuse food and shelter to a starving hunted
human being, but also should assist, if
called upon by the authorities, to seize the
unhappy fugitive and send him back to
slavery.

Their former owners sent slave catchers armed
with warrants for their immediate arrest, but they
were not taken into custody because a friend, the
Reverend Samuel May, arranged for them to move
to England. Their old owners, learning how the
Massachusetts authorities treated their agents,
wrote to Millard Fillmore, then president of the
United States, asking for help in returning them to
slavery. "Mr. Fillmore said that we should be

returned. He gave instructions for military force to be sent to Boston to assist the officers in making the arrest." President Fillmore's instructions arrived too late; the Crafts had already left for England.

Rev. Noah Davis
1859

The *Narrative of the Life of Rev. Noah Davis, a Colored Man* was published in Baltimore in 1859.[13] Noah Davis was born in Madison County, Virginia, March 1804. His father and his family belonged to Robert Patten, "a wealthy merchant, residing in Fredericksburg—who was also the owner . . . of a large merchant mill . . . ." Mr. Patten "was considered one of the best of masters, allowing his servants many privileges; but my father enjoyed more than many others."

His father, who was the head miller, had the rare privilege of keeping his children with him. "My oldest brother worked in the mill, with my father, while my youngest brother and I did little else than play about home and wait upon our mother."

His parents were members of the Baptist church. On Sundays, his father would "spend his time instructing his children, or the neighboring servants, out of the New Testament sent to him from Fredericksburg by one of his older sons."

Noah's pleasant life did not last long because Robert Patten and his partner decided to sell the mill and the farm. The owners freed Noah's father (but not Noah), and the family moved to another farm where Noah worked part of the time for a carpenter. When he was fourteen years old, Noah was sent from his home to apprentice under a shoemaker in Fredericksburg, Virginia.

In December 1818, for the first time in my life, I left home; and I was sad at the thought of parting with those whom I loved and reverenced more than any persons on earth. But the expectation of seeing Fredericksburg, a place which, from all I had then learned, I supposed must be the greatest place in the world, reconciled me somewhat with the necessity of saying goodbye to the dear ones at home. I arrived at Fredericksburg, after a day and a half's travel, in a wagon—a distance of some fifty miles. Having arrived in town, a boy green from the country, I was astonished and delighted at what appeared to me the splendor and beauty of the place. I spent a merry Christmas at my old master's stately mansion, along with my older brother, and for a while forgot the home on the farm.

Noah was to serve his apprenticeship with Mr. Thomas Wright, but before he began, he had to spend his first year as a house servant in Wright's home. In any case, his fondest wish was to learn to read and write. Fortunately his father had taught him the alphabet before he left the mill. After Noah became religious, he would carry his father's New Testament to church.

. . . And always try to get to meeting in time to hear the preacher read a chapter before sermon. If he named the chapter before reading it, I would soon find it. In this way, I gathered much information in pronouncing many hard words in the scripture. It was a long time before I learned the meaning of the numeral letters put in the Bible over the chapters. I had often seen them in the spelling book running alongside a column of figures; but no one ever told me that they were put there for the same . . . as the figures.

Later, he learned to write by imitating his employer. The shoemaker "used to write the names of his customers on the lining of the boots and shoes, as he gave them out to be made. So I tried to make letters, and soon succeeded in writing my name, and then the word Fredericksburg, and so on."

At length, Noah promised God that he would devote his life to preaching, and he was baptized "in company with some twenty others, by Rev. Geo. F. Adams, who was then pastor of the Baptist church in Fredericksburg—September 19, 1831." At this church, he formed an attachment to a young woman who had been baptized with him and whom he hoped to marry.

But we were both slaves, and of course, had to get the consent of our owners, before we went further. My wife belonged to the late Carter L. Stephenson, Esquire, who was a brother to the Honorable Andrew Stephenson of Virginia. My wife's master was quite indulgent to the servants about the house. He never restrained visitors from coming on his premises to visit his domestics. It was said he had the likeliest set of servant girls in town; and though I cannot say I got the prettiest, yet I think I got the best one among them. We have had nine children—seven born in slavery, and two since my wife's freedom. Five out of the seven in slavery I have bought—two are still in bondage.

Now married and a member of the church, Davis asked his owner, Patten, permission to purchase his freedom and to travel to raise the necessary funds. "He granted my request, without a single objection, fixing my price at five hundred dollars . . . and told me, when I got ready to start, he would give me a pass, to go where I pleased."

On June 1, 1841, Noah travelled to Philadelphia, New York, and Boston. However, he raised only one hundred fifty dollars.

The cause of my failure to raise all the money, I believe, was that I was unaccustomed to addressing large congregations of strangers; and often, when I was favored with an opportunity of presenting my case to the people, I would feel such embarrassment that I could scarcely say anything. And I met another obstacle, which discouraged me very much, which was that some persons would tell me they sympathized with me, in my efforts to get free; but they said it was against their principles to give money to buy slaves. I confess this was new to me, and would cut me down much in my spirits—still I found generous and noble-hearted friends, who treated me with every mark of kindness.

However, he did not stay downhearted for very long because he received a message from the pastor of his Fredericksburg church. A group of white Baptists in Baltimore wanted to hire him as a missionary to the black population there. They would also help him to raise the balance of the money owed to his owner.

This was indeed an unexpected, and to me an undesired call. I began to think how can I leave my wife and seven small children to go to Baltimore to live, a distance of more than a hundred miles from them. This, I thought, could not be. I thought my children would need my watchful care, more now than at any other time. It is true, they were all slaves, belonging to a rich widow lady. But she had always given me the entire control of my family. Now, if I should leave them at their tender age, mischief might befall them. Still, as the letter from Baltimore was from gentlemen of the best standing, it became me to give them an answer. This I could not do, without first consulting my master. I did so, and after giving the matter careful consideration, he thought I had better go and see those gentlemen—he was perfectly willing to leave the matter to me.

The result was that I accepted the offer of the brethren in Baltimore; and by them I was enabled to pay the debt I owed; and I have never had cause to repent it—though I had misgivings sometimes, when I would get into trouble.

His first year in Baltimore was very discouraging. There were few black Baptists. The black people in Baltimore were not friendly. He became aware that he was far behind them in education.

I had never had a day's schooling and coming to one of the first cities in the Union, where the colored people had the advantage of schools, and where their pulpits were occupied, Sabbath after Sabbath, by comparatively intelligent colored ministers—what could I expect, but that the people would turn away from one who was trying to preach in the room of a private house, some fifteen by twenty feet? Yet, there was no turning back; God had called me to the work, and it was His cause I was advocating.

I found that to preach, like other preachers, I must improve my mind, by reading the Bible and other good books, and by studying my own language. I started afresh—I got a small stock of books, and the white brethren loaned and gave me other useful volumes, to which they added a word of instruction and encouragement, whenever an opportunity offered; and the ministers cordially invited me to attend their Monday ministerial conference meeting, which was very useful to me.

By the end of his first year in Baltimore, Davis had arranged with the widow who owned his wife and children to purchase them for eight hundred dollars. Although the widow gave him twelve months in which to raise the money, the year passed and still Davis did not have the total. At the end of the year when he had not raised the money, the owner increased the amount. Mr. Wright under whom he had apprenticed told him, "Go get your wife; and you can keep on collecting, and repay the two hundred dollars when you get able."

By November 5, 1851, his wife and two of his children were with him in Baltimore. But he still had two problems facing him. One was to increase the membership of his church and the other was the fear that his children who remained in bondage would be sold.

> The first of these, who about to be sold and taken away South, was my oldest daughter; and it was with great difficulty and the help of friends that I raised eight hundred and fifty dollars, and got her on to Baltimore. But I was soon called upon to make a similar effort to save my eldest son from being sold far from me. Entirely unexpected, I received the painful news that my boy was in one of the trader's jails in Richmond, and for sale. The dealer knew me, and was disposed to let me have him, if I could get any one to purchase him. I was, of course, deeply anxious to help my boy; but I began to think that I had already drawn so heavily on the liberality of all my friends, that to appeal to them again seemed out of the question. I immediately wrote to the owners of my son,

and received an answer—that his price was fixed at seven hundred dollars.

Again, Davis began traveling to raise money with which to buy his children, but was unsuccessful. He prayed and thought until the idea occurred to him to write his autobiography.

The question then occurred to me, Could I not, by making a book, do something to relieve myself and my children, and ultimately, by the same means, help my church, under its heavy debt, also relieve the Missionary Board from helping me. This idea struck me with so much force, that I have yielded to it—that is, to write a short Narrative of my own life, setting forth the trials and difficulties the Lord has brought me through to this day, and offer it for sale to my friends generally, as well as to the public at large; and I hope it may not only aid me, but may serve to encourage others, who meet with similar difficulties, to put their trust in God.

Nat Love
1907

In the late nineteenth and early twentieth century many African-Americans published accounts of their times in slavery. *The Adventures of Nat Love* is an example of this revival of the slave narrative.[14] The exploits of Love, who had been born in slavery, is a rare memoir by a black cowboy.

Nat Love was born in Davidson County, Tennessee in June 1854. "The exact date of my birth I never knew, because in those days no count was kept of such trivial matters as the birth of a slave baby." Nat grew up practically alone as his parents' first obligation was to their work on the plantation and not to their children.

Since he was unsupervised as a child, Nat got into a great deal of trouble. Once his mother made some wine and left it in the garden to ferment. The children discovered the wine and drank all of it. After finishing the jug, they passed out. Nat explains, "I suppose I acquired the taste for strong drink on this occasion; be that as it may, the fact remains that I could outdrink any man I ever met in the cattle country."

Nat's narrative is not limited to his experiences in slavery or his life in the West. He also explains how the South and perhaps the country became rich and powerful based on slave labor.

> . . . On the plantations all around us were thousands of slaves, all engaged in garnering the dollars that kept up the so-called aristocracy of the South, and many of the proud old families owe their standing and wealth to the toil and sweat of the black man's brow, where if they had to pay the regular rate of wages to hire laborers to cultivate their large estates, their wealth would not have amounted to a third of what it was. Wealth was created, commerce carried on, cities built, and the new world well started on the career that has led to its present greatness and standing in the world of nations. All this was accomplished by the sweat of the black man's brow. By black man I do not mean to say only the black man, but the black woman and black child all helped to make the proud South what it was. . . .

The Civil War broke out when Nat was about ten years old. When Lee surrendered, both Nat's owner and his father returned from the war. "But in common with other masters of those days he [the owner] did not tell us we were free. And instead of letting us go he made us work for him the same as before. . . ." Nat's father died shortly after returning from the war. His father's death and the subsequent death of his brother-in-law caused Nat to see himself as the head of the family. To support his family, Nat went to work. Not far from his cabin was a horse ranch where the owner, Mr. Williams, gave Nat ten cents for every colt that he broke.

In February 1869, with the experience he had gained working for Mr. Williams, Nat Love, at the age of fifteen, left home. He struck out for Kansas because it was in the West and it was the West that he wanted to see. In Dodge City, Kansas, he was offered a job if he could break a horse. He was successful and the boss offered him a job paying thirty dollars per month. "He asked what my name was and I answered Nat Love. He said to the boys we will call him Red River Dick. I went by this name for a long time."

This group of cowboys was originally from Texas. After Nat got the job, they returned to Texas. Along the way, they encountered a band of Indians.

> This was my first Indian fight and likewise the first Indians I had ever seen. When I saw them coming after us and heard their bloodcurdling yell, I lost all courage and thought my time had come to die. I was too badly scared to run. Some of the boys told me to use my gun and shoot for all I was worth . . . after the first shot I lost all fear and fought like a veteran.

Soon the cowboys routed them, but not before the Indians had taken everything that the cowboys had.

The home ranch was located on the Palo Duro

River in the western part of the Texas panhandle. Nat Love worked there as a cowboy for about three years until he accepted another position in Arizona. His skill in riding, roping, and in the general routine of the cowboy's life, including his knowledge of the surrounding country, gained from many long trips with herds of cattle and horses, made him an especially valued employee.

Until 1875 he was known all over the West as "Red River Dick," a name that his first boss had given him in Kansas. By 1876, however, he won the name of Deadwood Dick, "a name I made even better known than Red River Dick."

> The name of Deadwood Dick was given to me by the people of Deadwood, South Dakota, July 4, 1876, after I had proven myself worthy to carry it, and after I had defeated all comers in riding, roping, and shooting, and I have always carried the name with honor since that time.

It was also in 1876 that the ranch for which he worked received orders to deliver three thousand head of cattle to Deadwood, South Dakota. Nat was not the only African-American cowboy on the cattle drive; there were approximately six others. The cowboys had not been on the trail for very long before they met other outfits who told them that General Custer was out after the Indians.

> . . . A big fight was expected when the Seventh U.S. Cavalry . . . met the Crow tribe, and other Indians under the leadership of Sitting Bull, Rain-in-the-Face, Old Chief Joseph, and other chiefs of lesser

prominence, who had for a long time been terrorizing the settlers of that section and defying the Government."

When the Indians finally met the Cavalry in the Little Big Horn basin, Nat Love and his group were about two days behind them, or within sixty miles. Nat Love did not know of the battle until several days after it was over. On his way back from the cattle drive, after the Battle of the Little Big Horn, Love met and talked with many famous government scouts, Buffalo Bill (William F. Cody), Yellow Stone Kelley, and others.

On October 4, 1876, while riding alone, hunting strays, Indians attacked, wounded, and captured Nat. Nat speculates why his life was spared.

> What caused them to spare my life I cannot tell, but it was I think partly because I had proved myself a brave man, and all savages admire a brave man and when they captured a man whose fighting powers were out of the ordinary they generally kept him, if possible, as he was needed in the tribe.

He speculates further.

> . . . Yellow Dog's tribe was composed largely of half breeds, and there was a large percentage of colored blood in the tribe, and as I was a colored man they wanted to keep me, as they thought I was too good a man to die.

The chief offered Love his daughter as his wife. With her came a dowry of one hundred ponies. However, Nat was not anxious to be married under those circumstances at that particular time. One night he escaped.

Later, Nat went on another cattle drive to Dodge City, Kansas. He passed Fort Dodge and decided to rope a cannon and take it back to Texas with him. "The bad whiskey which I carried under my belt was responsible for the fool idea, and gave me the nerve to attempt to execute the idea." As the cannon was too heavy for his horse to pull, the military authorities apprehended and jailed him. Nat told the guard that he knew Bat Masterson. The commanding officer took him into the city to see Masterson.

> As soon as Masterson saw me he asked me what the trouble was, and before I could answer, the guards told him I rode into the fort and roped one of the cannons and tried to pull it out. Bat asked me what I wanted with a cannon and what I intended doing with it. I told him I wanted to take it back to Texas with me to fight the Indians with; then they all laughed.

Later, while on a cattle drive to Cheyenne, Wyoming, Nat saw "considerable of William H. Bonney alias 'Billy the Kid,' the most noted desperado and all around bad man the world has known." Nat first met The Kid in Antonshico, New Mexico, in 1877. He met Billy the Kid several more times before The Kid's death. The last time he saw The Kid he was "laying dead at Pete Maxwell's ranch in Lincoln County, New Mexico, having been killed by Pat A. Garret, at that time sheriff of Lincoln County, New Mexico." Nat Love asks the reader not to condemn Billy. "He had many traits that go to make a good man, but fate and circumstances were

111

against the kid. . . ." Other bad men Nat met during his travels in the West were the James brothers, Frank and Jesse. Nat describes them as "true men, brave, kind, generous and considerate."

At the time of the writing of his narrative, Nat Love was employed by the General Securities Company in Los Angeles.

> Life today on the cattle range is almost another epoch. Laws have been enacted in Mew Mexico and Arizona which forbid all the old-time sports and the cowboy is almost a being of the past. But, I, Nat Love, now in my 54th year, hale, hearty and happy, will ever cherish a fond and loving feeling for the old days on the range, its exciting adventures, good horses, good and bad men, long venturesome rides, Indian fights and last but foremost the friends I have made and friends I have gained.

The Oral Accounts
of Ex-Slaves
1938

In the 1930s the federal government sent journalists, writers, and folklorists to collect the memories of ex-slaves, who were dying out. The following narratives are reproduced exactly as they appear in government files.[15]

AMBROSE DOUGLASS

In 1861, when he was sixteen years old, Ambrose Hilliard Douglass was given a sound beating by his North Carolina master because he attempted to refuse the mate that had been given to him with the instructions to produce a healthy boy-child by her—and a long argument on the value of having good, strong, healthy children. In 1937, at the age of 92, Ambrose Douglass welcomed his 38th child into the world.

The near-centennarian [sic] lives near Brooksville in Hernando County [Florida], on a rundown farm that he no longer attempts to tend now that most of his 38 children have deserted the farm for the more lucrative employment of the cities or the phosphate camps.

Douglass was born free in Detroit in 1845. His parents returned South to visit relatives still in slavery, and were soon reenslaved themselves, with their children. Ambrose was one of these.

For 21 years he remained in slavery, sometimes at the plantation of his original master in North Carolina, sometimes in other sections after he had been sold to different masters.

"Yassuh, I been sold a lot of times," the old man states. "Our master didn't believe in keeping a house, a horse or a darky. . . . I was sold when I cut up.

"I was a young man," he continues, "and didn't see why I should be anybody's slave. I'd run away every chance I got. Sometimes they near killed me, but mostly they just sold me. I guess I was pretty husky, at that.

"They never did get their money's worth out of me, though I worked as long as they stood over me, then I ran around with the gals or sneaked off to the woods. Sometimes they used to put dogs on me to get me back.

"When they finally sold me to a man up in Suwannee County [Florida]—his name was Harris—I thought it would be the end of the world. We had heard about him all the way up in Virginia. They said he beat you, starved you and tied you up when you didn't work, and killed you if you ran away.

"But I never had a better master. He never beat me, and always fed all of us. Course, we didn't get too much to eat; corn meal, a little piece of fat meat now and then, cabbages, greens, potatoes, and plenty of molasses. When I worked at "the house" I et just what the master et; sometimes he would give it to me his-self. When he didn't I et it anyway.

"He was so good, and I was so scared of him, till I didn't ever run away from his place," Ambrose reminisces. "I had somebody there that I liked, anyway. When he finally went to the war he sold me back to a man in North Carolina, in Hornett County. But the war was near over then; I soon was as free as I am now.

"I guess we musta celebrated 'Mancipation about twelve times in Hornett County. Every time a bunch of No'thern sojers would come through they would tell us we was free and we'd begin celebratin'. Before we would get through somebody else would tell us to go back to work, but we didn't know who was goin' to win and didn't take no chances.

"I was 21 when freedom finally came, and that time I didn't take no chances on 'em taking it back again. I lit out for Florida and wound up in Madison County. I had a nice time there; I got married, got plenty of work, and made me a little money. I fixed houses, built 'em, worked around the yards, and did everything. My first child was already born; I didn't know there was goin' to be 37 more, though. I guess I would have stopped right there.

"I stayed in Madison County until they started to working concrete rock down here. I heard about it and thought that would be a good way for me to feed all them two dozen children I had. So I came down this side. That was about 20 years ago.

"I got married again after I got here; right soon after. My wife is now 30 years old; we already had 13 children together. (His wife is a slight, girlish-looking woman; she says she was 13 when she married Douglass, had her first child that year. Eleven

115

of her thirteen are still living.)

"Nossuh, I ain't long stopped work. I worked here in the phosphate mine until last year, when they started to paying pensions. I thought I would get one, but all I got was some PWA work, and this year they told me I was too old for that. I told 'em I wasn't but 91, but they didn't give nothin' else. I guess I'll get my pension soon, though. My oldest boy ought to get it, too; he's sixty-five.

WILLIAM P. HOGUE

"I was born a slave in Halifax County, Virginia, April 27, 1861. I really don't remember nothing about slavery, but I heard my mother and the older children tell about things what happened.

"They was seven of us; mother and father, and five of us children. I was named after my father, William P. Hogue, and my mother's name was Grace. We was owned by Dr. P. Hogue. He had two plantations and a lot of slaves. He had a big fine house, setting in about 14 acres called the home farm. They raised a lot of corn, tobacco, and wheat and regular garden stuff, and cattle.

"Dr. Hogue had two sons in the Rebel army, and he used to press his slaves in the Rebel service to do the hard work, and be personal slaves for his boys. Father was pressed into the Rebel army, and he died before he came back.

"After the war we stayed on for a few years on Dr. Hogue's place, then we moved further out in the country on a place of our own. I finally moved up to Paris, Kentucky, where I married and all five of my children was born here. I moved to Springfield about 25 years ago.

"I didn't get much chance to go to school. I remember I had a book one day when we was on

Dr. Hogue's place, and I got a whipping, and they done told me, don't never let me catch me with a book again. 'Bout two years ago I went to the 'Mergency School, and I learned to read and figure real well, and now I can entertain my ownself by reading and writing, and kind of do my own figuring.

"I use to know lots of tales and superstition, but I don't recollect any just off hand, because my memory ain't as good as it used to be, no how.

DOUGLAS DORSEY

In South Jacksonville, on the Spring Glen Road lives Douglas Dorsey, an ex-slave, born in Suwanee County, Florida in 1851, fourteen years prior to freedom. His parents Charlie and Anna Dorsey were natives of Maryland and free people. In those days, Dorsey relates there were people known as "Nigger Traders" who used any subterfuge to catch Negroes and sell them into slavery. There was one Jeff Davis who was known as a professional "Nigger Trader," his slave boat docked in the slip at Maryland and Jeff Davis and his henchmen went out looking for their victims. Unfortunately, his mother Anna and his father were caught one night and were bound and gagged and taken to Jeff Davis' boat which was waiting in the harbor, and there they were put into the stocks. The boat stayed in port until it was loaded with Negroes, then sailed for Florida where Davis disposed of his human cargo.

Douglas Dorsey's parents were sold to Colonel Louis Matair, who had a large plantation that was cultivated by 85 slaves. Colonel Matair's house was of the pretentious southern colonial type that was quite prevalent during that period. The colonel had won his title because of his participation in the Indian War in Florida. He was the typical wealthy Southern gentleman, and was very kind to his slaves. His wife, however was just the opposite. She was exceedingly mean and could easily be termed a tyrant.

There were several children in the Matair family and their home and plantation were located in Suwannee County, Florida.

Douglas' parents were assigned to their tasks, his mother was housemaid and his father was the mechanic, having learned his trade in Maryland as a free man. Charlie and Anna had several children and Douglas was among them. When he became large enough he was kept in the Matair home to build fires, assist in serving meals and other chores.

Mrs. Matair being a very cruel woman would whip the slaves herself for any misdemeanor. Dorsey recalls an incident that is hard to obliterate from his mind; it is as follows: Dorsey's mother was called by Mrs. Matair. Not hearing her, she continued her duties. Suddenly Mrs. Matair burst out in a frenzy of anger over the woman not answering. Anna explained that she did not hear her call; thereupon Mrs. Matair seized a large butcher knife and struck at Anna. Attempting to ward off the blow, Anna received a long gash on the arm that laid her up for some time. Young Douglas was a witness to this brutal treatment of his mother and he at that moment made up his mind to kill his mistress. He intended to put strychnine—that was used to kill rats—into her coffee that he usually served her. Fortunately, freedom came and saved him from doing this act which would have resulted in his death.

He relates another incident in regard to his

mistress as follows: To his mother and father was born a little baby boy, whose complexion was rather light. Mrs. Matair at once began accusing Colonel Matair as being the father of the child. Naturally the Colonel denied it, but Mrs. Matair kept harassing him about it until he finally agreed to his wife's desire and sold the child. It was taken from its mother's breast at the age of eight months and auctioned off on the first day of January to the highest bidder. The child was bought by a Captain Ross and taken across the Suwanee River into Hamilton County. Twenty years later he was located by his family; he was a grown man, married and farming.

Young Douglas had the task each morning of carrying the Matair children's books to school. Willie, a boy of eight, would teach Douglas what he learned in school; finally Douglas learned the alphabet and numbers. In some way Mrs. Matair learned that Douglas was learning to read and write. One morning after breakfast she called her son Willie to the dining room where she was seated and they sent for Douglas to come there, too. She then took a quill pen, the kind used at that time, and began writing the alphabet and numerals as far as ten. Holding the paper up to Douglas, she asked him if he knew what they were; he proudly answered in the affirmative, not suspecting anything. She then asked him to name the letters and numerals, which he did, she then asked him to write them, which he did. When he reached the number ten, very proud of his learning, she struck him a heavy blow across the face, saying to him, "If I ever catch you making another figure anywhere I'll cut off your right arm." Naturally Douglas and also her son Willie were much surprised as each thought what had been done was quite an achievement. She then called Mariah, the cook, to bring a rope and tying the two of them to the old colonial post on the front porch, she took a chair and sat between the two whipping them on their naked backs for such a time, that for two weeks their clothes stuck to their backs on the lacerated flesh.

To ease the soreness, Willie would steal grease from the house and together they would slip into the barn and grease each other's backs.

As to plantation life, Dorsey said that the slaves lived in quarters especially built for them on the plantation. They would leave for the fields at "sun up" and remain until "sundown," stopping only for a meal which they took along with them.

Instead of having an overseer they had what was called a "driver" by the name of January. His duties were to get the slaves together in the morning and see that they went to the fields and assign them to their tasks. He worked as the other slaves, though he had more privileges. He would stop work at any time he pleased and go around to inspect the work of the others, and thus rest himself. Most of the orders from the master were issued to him. The crops consisted of cotton, corn, cane and pease, which was raised in abundance.

When the slaves left the fields, they returned to their cabins and after preparing and eating of their evening meal they gathered around a cabin to sing and moan songs seasoned with African melody. Then to the tune of an old fiddle they danced a dance called the "Green Corn Dance" and "Cut the Pigeon Wing." Sometimes the young men on the plantation would slip away to visit a girl on another plantation. If they were caught by the "Patrols" while on these visits they would be lashed on their bare backs as a penalty for the offense.

A whipping post was used for this purpose. As soon as one slave was whipped, he was given the whip to whip his brother slave. Very often the lashes would bring blood very soon from the already lacerated skin, but this did not stop the lashing until one had received their due number of lashes.

Occasionally the slaves were ordered to church to hear a white minister; they were seated in the front pews of the master's church, while the whites sat in the rear. The minister's admonition to them [was] to honor their masters and mistresses, and to have no other God before them, as "we cannot see the other God, but you can see your master and mistress." After the services the driver's wife who could read and write a little would tell them that what the minister said "was all lies."

Douglas says that he will never forget—when he was a lad of 14 years of age—when one evening he was told to go and tell the driver to have all the slaves come up to the house; soon the entire host of about 85 slaves were gathered there, all sitting around on stumps, some standing. The colonel's son was visibly moved as he told them they were free. Saying they could go anywhere they wanted to for he had no more to do with them or that they could remain with him and have half of what was raised on the plantation.

The slaves were happy at this news, as they had hardly been aware that there had been a war going on. None of them accepted the offer of the colonel to remain, as they were only too glad to leave the cruelties of the Matair Plantation.

Dorsey's father got a job with Judge Carraway of Suwanee where he worked for one year. He later homesteaded 40 acres of land that he received from the government and began farming. Dorsey's father died in Suwanee County, Florida, when Douglass was a young man and then he and his mother moved to Arlington, Florida. His mother died several years ago at a ripe old age.

Sources

1. Excerpts from *The History of Mary Prince, a West Indian Slave. Related by Herself. To which is added the Narrative of Asa-Asa, A Captured African.* London: F. Westley and A.H. Davis, 1831.

2. Excerpts from Moses Roper, *A Narrative of Moses Roper's Adventures and Escape from American Slavery; with a Preface by Reverend T. Price.* Philadelphia: Merrihew and Gunn, 1838.

3. Excerpts from Lewis Williamson, "The Story of Lewis Williamson. As Related by Himself." *The Colored American*, November 13, 1841.

4. Excerpts from Frederick Douglass, *Narrative of the Life of Frederick Douglass, An American Slave. Written by Himself.* First published in the United States by The Anti-Slavery Office 1845.

5. Excerpts from William Wells Brown, *Narrative of William Wells Brown, Fugitive Slave.* Boston: Anti-Slavery Office, 1847.

6. Excerpts from Henry Bibb, *Narrative of the Life and Adventures of Henry Bibb, An American Slave, Written by Himself.* New York: self-published manuscript, 1849.

7. Excerpts from Henry Box Brown, *Narrative of the Life of Henry Box Brown, Written By Himself*. First English Edition. Manchester, England: Lee and Glynn, 1851.

8. Excerpts from Josiah Henson, *"Truth Is Stranger Than Fiction." An Autobiography of the Rev. Josiah Henson*. Boston: B.B. Russell & Co., 1879.

9. James Smith, "The Lost Is Found," *Voice of the Fugitive*, Sandwich, Canada West, Jan. 15, Feb. 25, March 11, April 2, April 22, 1852.

10. "A Short and True Story of a Fugitive," *The Provincial Freeman*, Chatham, Canada West, August 29, 1855.

11. Excerpts from Solomon Northup, *Twelve Years a Slave. Narrative of Solomon Northup, a Citizen of New York, kidnapped in Washington City in 1841, and Rescued in 1853, from a Cotton Plantation near the Red River, in Louisiana*. Auburn: Derby and Miller, Buffalo: Derby, Orton and Mulligan, Cincinnati: Henry W. Derby, 1853.

12. Excerpts from William and Ellen Craft, *Running a Thousand Miles for Freedom, or the Escape of William and Ellen Craft from Slavery*. London: William Tweedie, 1860.

13. Excerpts from Noah Davis, *A Narrative of the Life of Reverend Noah Davis, a Colored Man, Written by Himself*. Baltimore: J.F. Weishampel, Jr., 1859.

14. Excerpts from Nat Love, *The Life and Adventures of Nat Love, Better Known in The Cattle Country as "Deadwood Dick." By Himself. A True History of Slavery Days, Life on the Great Cattle Ranges and on the Plains of the "Wild and Wooly" West, Based on Facts, and Personal Experiences of the Author*. Los Angeles: Nat Love, 1907.

15. *Oral Narratives of the Ex Slaves, The Ohio Project*, WPA, 1938 from the Schomberg Collection, New York Public Library, N.Y.

Suggested Reading

Alford, Terry. *Prince among Slaves*. New York: Oxford University Press, 1977.

Betts, Robert B. *In Search of York: The Slave Who Went with Lewis and Clark*. Boulder: Colorado Associated University Press, 1985.

Clayton, Ronnie W. *Mother Wit: the Ex-slaves Narratives of the Louisiana Writers' Project*. New York: P. Lang, 1990.

Curtin, Phillip, ed. *Africa Remembered, Narratives by West Africans from the Era of the Slave Trade*. Madison: University of Wisconsin Press, 1967.

Davis, Charles T. and Henry Louis Gates, Jr. *The Slave's Narrative*. New York: Oxford University Press, 1985.

Mellon, James, ed. *Bullwhip Days: the Slaves Remember*. New York: Weidenfeld and Nicholson, 1988.

Nichols, Charles Harold. *Many Thousands Gone; the Ex-slaves' Account of Their Bondage and Freedom*. Leiden: Brill, 1963.

Teamoh, George. *God Made Man, Man Made the Slave: The Autobiography of George Teamoh*. Macon, Ga.: Mercer, 1990.

Thomas, James P. *From Tennessee Slave to St. Louis Entrepreneur*. Columbia: University of Missouri Press, 1984.

Index